Stirling Castle

Its Place in Scotland's History, in Battle, and in the Lives of Scottish Kings and Queens

By Eric Stair-Kerr

Illustrated by Hugh Armstrong Cameron

PANTIANOS
CLASSICS

Published by Pantianos Classics

ISBN-13: 978-1-78987-178-4

First published in 1913

Contents

Preface

Stirling Castle is a many-sided subject that can be treated in more than one way. The story of the castle might be dealt with in a book divided into sections, each one taking up a special part, such as Military History, Stirling as a Royal Palace, Notable Visitors, etc.; but I have thought it better to set forth the whole of the castle's history in chronological order, and, after discussing the buildings and their associations, to bring together the salient events connected with the three chief Scottish strongholds, and to record what the poets have said about Stirling.

With regard to dates, for the sake of simplicity I have adopted the historical computation; that is to say, the years have been reckoned as if they had always begun on the 1st of January and not on the 25th of March, as was the rule in Scotland until 1600. For example, the date of Prince Henry's birth is given as February, 1594, although the event was considered at the time to belong to the year 1593.

I am glad to express here my thanks to my uncle, the Rev. Eric Robertson, for suggesting that I should undertake this work, and for valuable hints given from time to time; to Mr. David B. Morris, Stirling, who has always responded most willingly to any appeal for help, and who has kindly read the proofs; and to Mr. James Hyslop, Edinburgh, for guidance in the subject of the buildings of the castle. To the artist, Mr. Cameron, I am grateful for the whole-hearted interest which he has taken in my part of the work as well as in his own.

E. S. K.

Chapter One - Early History

For many centuries travellers have been struck by the remarkable resemblance which Stirling bears to Edinburgh. In each case there is a castle perched on a precipitous rock, and a town built on a narrow ridge that slopes from the crag to the plain. That two places so much alike in situation should be found in Scotland, and but thirty miles apart, may seem a matter for wonder, but a word or two on the geology of the district may help to explain how the similarity arose.

During the Great Ice Age, when the physical features of Scotland were moulded into almost their present form, the extensive plain of the River Forth was filled by a giant glacier, which swept down from the Highland hills to the lower land on the south and east, clearing the softer rocks from its path and exposing the hard basalt of igneous sheets and old volcanic necks. These great eruptive obstructions withstood the pressure of the eastward-moving mass of ice, and so prevented the ground on their lee sides from being subjected to the scouring action that hollowed out the land on the north and west and south. Numerous examples of this "crag and tail" formation are to be found in the track of the ancient glacier, but two of the rocks stand out with striking prominence; on one is built the Castle of Edinburgh, on the other that of Stirling.

It is strange that of such natural strongholds early history has so little to say, for these fortresses were afterwards to have their names writ large on almost every page of Scotland's romantic story. The third sister castle, Dumbarton, came earlier to the front. It was a stronghold of renown in the days of the Strathclyde Britons; but as time wore on its importance diminished, and the place which it had held in the principality of Strathclyde was taken by Stirling and Edinburgh in the consolidated Kingdom of Scotland.

On the Gowan Hills, to the north of Stirling Castle, traces of an ancient fort show that the Britons considered it more important to defend the rising ground overlooking the River Forth than to occupy the crag, with its precipitous south-west face. When the Romans under Agricola attempted the conquest of northern Britain they constructed a chain of forts across the country, between the Firths of Forth and Clyde. The untrustworthy Boece asserts that Stirling was fortified at the time of those campaigns, but no real traces of their work have been discovered to prove that the Romans occupied the castle rock under Agricola in A.D. 81–82, or when Lollius Urbicus, Governor of Britain for Antoninus Pius, erected the wall on the line of the earlier forts. Near the Pass of Ballengeich is the so-called Roman Stone, with its indistinct, almost unintelligible letters. Antiquaries of a former day—Camden, Sibbald and Horsley—considered the inscription genuine, but recent scholars are of opinion that the letters were carved many centuries after the departure of the legions from Britain. Again, the existence of a Roman causeway has not yet been proved. The natural supposition that a military road, connecting the camp at Ardoch with the south, passed near Stirling led to the belief that the highway crossed the Forth at Kildean, or higher up at the Ferry of Drip. No vestiges of a causeway of undoubted Roman origin have, however, been discovered either at the river or on the Field of Bannockburn, through which it was thought to have passed on its way to the station of Camelon.

After the withdrawal of the Roman legions, Stirling Castle dimly appears in the haze of half-real history. King Arthur is claimed as a local prince in Brittany, Cornwall, Wales and Cumberland, but southern Scotland seems to have, on the whole, the best right to the hero of romance. His tenth battle, it would seem, was fought in the neighbourhood of Stirling, and his victory over the Saxons gave him possession of the fortress. Tradition has always associated his name with the Round Table, which afterwards became the King's Knot, and William of Worcester, who flourished in the fifteenth century, wrote that King Arthur preserved the Round Table in the Castle of Stirling or Snowden. [1]

A less famous, though not a less real, person than the great British warrior chief was Monenna or Modwenna, a high-born saint of Ireland. At least two women bearing this name devoted themselves to the religious life, and some confusion has arisen as to which of them it was who became connected with Stirling. The Monenna who lived in the ninth century, however, apparently visited both England and Scotland, and she seems to have been the one who built, among other churches, the chapel in Stirling Castle. [2]

Perhaps because the fortress was so obviously a place of strength the early chroniclers have associated with it events which possibly never took place. Boece mentions that Kenneth MacAlpine laid siege to the castle during the Pictish wars; and the same historian asserts that King Osbert of Northumbria occupied Stirling for a number of years, and established a mint in the fortress. A "cunyie-house" at one time did exist in the castle, but the oldest coins known to have been struck at Stirling date from the reign of Alexander III. A site so favourable for a stronghold, however, must have been the scene of many unrecorded fights, so that "the place of striving," which was formerly thought to have been the meaning of the citadel's name, would be no inappropriate appellation. "Stirling" is now held to be a corruption of the Welsh *Ystre Felyn*, signifying "The dwelling of Velin," old forms of the name being *Estrevelyn*, *Striviling* and *Struelin*. [3] The more poetic "Snowdon" or "Snawdoun," a corruption perhaps of some Celtic appellation, or else meaning merely the "snowy hill," was the name given to Stirling by some of the old chroniclers, as well as by Sir David Lyndsay in *The Testament of the Papingo*.

As Rutherglen is known as Ruglen, as Anstruther is called Anster, so Striviling throughout the ages has been spoken of as Stirling. Scots have always had a tendency to elide a syllable or to soften any harshness in their place-names, and the metathesis of the letter *r* and its vowel is common in the English language, as in the case of *three, third* and *hundred*, which used to be

6

sounded as *hunderd*. In modern times the spelling of the name has been fixed to suit the pronunciation, but that in James IV.'s reign the place was called Stirling is seen from the rhyming lines of one of Dunbar's poems:

"Cum hame and dwell no moir in Striuilling;Frome hiddouss hell cum hame and dwell,Quhair fische to sell is non bot spirling;Cum hame and dwell no moir in Striuilling." [4]

In the poems of Barbour and Wyntoun the scansion seems to require the name to be pronounced as a word of two syllables, and in Sir David Lyndsay's *Complaynt* the following lines occur:

"Quhen his Grace cumis to fair SterlingThere sall he se ane dayis derling."

Definite though meagre history associated with Stirling begins with the reign of Alexander I., who occupied the Scottish throne from 1107 till 1124. This monarch, known as "The Fierce," because of his swift vengeance on the rebellious subjects who rose to attack him at Invergowrie, seems to have frequently resided in the castle. He apparently built a new chapel on the rock, for during the reign of his brother David a document, drawn up at Edinburgh to settle a dispute concerning tithes, refers to the dedication by King Alexander of the Chapel of Stirling Castle:

"Hec est concordia que facta fuit apud Castellum Puellarum, coram rege Dauid et filio eius et baronibus eorum, inter R. episcopum Sancti Andree et G. abbatem de Dunfermelyn, de ecclesia parochiali de Eccles et Capella Castelli de Striuelin: Recordati fuerunt barones regis, et in hac recordacione omnes concordati sunt, quod ea die que Rex Alexander facit Capellam dedicare supra dictam, donauit et concessit eidem Capelle decimas dominiorum suorum in soca de Striuelin; que eadem die fuerunt domina sua siue acreuerunt siue decreuerunt...." [5]

The above may be rendered as follows in English:

"This is the agreement that was made at the Castle of the Maidens [Edinburgh] in the presence of King David, his son Henry and their barons, between Robert, Bishop of St. Andrews, and Galfrid, Abbot of Dunfermline, regarding the parish church of Eccles and the chapel of Stirling Castle. The King's barons remembered, and in that remembrance all agreed, that on the day on which King Alexander dedicated the aforesaid chapel, he gave and granted to it the tithes of his domains in the jurisdiction of Stirling, which domains were his at the time, whether they increased or decreased."

Although given the name of "The Fierce" by his subjects, Alexander was not of an irreligious temperament. From Queen Margaret, his mother, he inherited an interest in ecclesiastical affairs, and although he was not such a lavish patron of the clergy as was his brother David, he to some extent remodelled the Scottish Church. Alexander died in Stirling Castle, leaving the crown and a prosperous realm to David I., who made the fortress one of his chief residences, many of his charters being dated at "Striuelin." During the reign of the "sair sanct for the Croun," as David was called by his descendant, James I., the castle did not conspicuously figure in history; not till the time of William the Lion did it appear as a place of national importance. Then, however, its

7

name became prominent in the convention that brought Scotland's pride to a fall.

The Treaty of Falaise is the most humiliating document in the records of Scottish history. It proclaims the feudal subjection of Scotland to Henry II. of England. The circumstances leading to this unhappy situation may be briefly stated. Young Henry of England rebelled against his father, and procured the assistance of William the Lion by offering him Northumberland. The King of Scots accordingly swept across the Border, but was captured under the walls of Alnwick in 1174. The royal prisoner was taken by the English King to the Castle of Falaise in Normandy, where he lay in chains for several months till conditions of peace were arranged.

The terms of the treaty were that he, his brother, his barons and his clergy were to be vassals of Henry II., that the English Church was to exercise the rights which it was wont to claim over the Scottish Church, and, in order to ensure the fulfilment of the conditions, the castles of Roxburgh, Berwick, Jedburgh, Edinburgh and Stirling were to be garrisoned by English soldiers. [6] Henry, however, seems to have been satisfied with the occupation of Roxburgh, Berwick and Edinburgh, for when Richard I. fifteen years later acknowledged the independence of Scotland, he handed over only the two Tweedside fortresses, and made no mention of Jedburgh and Stirling. Edinburgh Castle was restored a few years earlier as the dower of Ermengarde de Beaumont, who, in compliance with the wishes of Henry II., married King William the Lion.

It is to the credit of the King of Scots that he adhered to the convention made at Falaise. When summoned he attended his suzerain's court, and even journeyed to Normandy to meet his lord. The terms of a treaty, although signed under compulsion, were held by William to be sacred, and his behaviour is in striking contrast to the conduct of the chivalry-loving Francis I. of France, who, when placed in similar circumstances three and a half centuries later, broke his oath to the Emperor Charles V. and renounced the Treaty of Madrid on the ground that a promise could not be binding when extorted from a reluctant prisoner.

King William added to the amenity of Stirling Castle by forming a royal park on the table-land to the south-west of the rock. In causing this enclosure to be made, he unwittingly trespassed on property belonging to the monks of Dunfermline, and the following deed of excambion shows the King's acknowledgment of the mistake and his readiness to give compensation to the abbey:

"Willelmus Rex Scottorum omnibus probis hominibus tocius terre sue, clericis laicis, salutem. Sciatis me concessisse et dedisse et hac carta me confirmasse Deo et ecclesie Sancte Trinitatis de Dunfermelyn et monachis ibidem Deo seruientibus et Capelle Castelli mei de Striuelin in excambium terre sue quam primum clausi in parco meo quando parcum meum primum clausi, terram que est inter terram suam quam habent extra parcum et diuisas terre de Kirketun et ex alia parte terram que est inter Cambusbarun

8

terram Petri de Striuelin et terram Rogeri filii Odonis, sicut magna strata uadit ad Cuiltedouenald, sicut Ricardus de Moreuilla, constabularius, et Robertus Auenel, justiciarius, et Radulphus vicecomes, et Petrus de Striuelin perambulaverunt: Tenendam in perpetuam elemosinam ita libere et quiete, sicut alias elemosinas suas tenent: Testibus, Ricardo de Moruilla, constabulario, Roberto Auenel, justiciario, Alano filio dapiferi, Adamo filio Thome, Rogero de Voloniis, Radulpho vicecomite de Striuelin, Petro de Striuelin, Waltero de Berkelai; Ricardo clerico apud Striuelin." [7]

THE HIGHLANDS FROM STIRLING CASTLE.

In English this runs as follows:

"William King of Scots to all good men of his whole realm greeting. Know that I have granted and given and by this charter have confirmed to God and the Church of the Holy Trinity at Dunfermline and the monks there serving God and to the Chapel of my Castle of Stirling in exchange for their land which I formerly included in my park, when I first enclosed my park, the land which is between their land which they have outside the park and the boundary of the land of Kirkton, and on the other side the land which is between Cambusbarron—the land of Peter of Stirling—and the land of Roger, son of Odo, as the highway leads to Cuiltedouenald, as Richard Morville, the constable, Robert Avenel, the justiciar, Ralph the sheriff and Peter of Stirling have marked it out: to be held in perpetual alms. Witnessed by Richard de Morville, constable, Robert Avenel, justiciar, Alan, son of the Steward, Adam, son of Thomas, Roger de Voloniis, Ralph, Sheriff of Stirling, Peter of Stirling, Walter de Berkeley, Richard the clerk, At Stirling."

In the later years of William the Lion war with England seemed likely to break out. The Scottish King would not relinquish his claim to Northumberland, for which he had offered Richard Cœur de Lion the sum of 15,000 merks, and John repeatedly declined to come to an agreement regarding the disputed territory. More than once William prepared for war, and in 1209 he

9

met his Great Council in Stirling Castle for the purpose of sending a deputation to lay the case once more before the English King. The result of this embassy was that the armies of both countries advanced towards the Border; but negotiations were again entered into before any fighting took place, so that peace was with difficulty preserved.

After reigning for nearly fifty years William the Lion began to realise that his powers were beginning to fail. During an expedition into the district of Moray his health completely broke down, but he felt that he might recover his strength if he were to breathe the invigorating air of Stirling. Slowly he made his journey southward, and succeeded in reaching his favourite seat, but the breezes of the Forth were no more restorative than the winds of the Spey or the Findhorn. [8] The aged monarch expired in the castle in December, 1214, bequeathing an independent kingdom to the youthful Alexander II., his only son by Ermengarde de Beaumont.

Under the new King, Stirling continued to benefit by the presence of the Court, and although no stirring history connected with the castle falls to be recorded of this prosperous reign, it should be mentioned that the King more than once held his Council or Parliament at Stirling, and doubtless the assembly met in a hall of the royal castle. Alexander III. followed his predecessors in making the lofty fortress one of his chosen homes, and once indeed, in the troubles of his early reign, he was compelled to take up residence within its walls. That incident occurred in 1257, during Alexander's minority, when two hostile parties of nobles struggled to obtain the control of the state. The Comyns—more patriotic than their opponents, who were ruling in the English interest—resolved to effect a change of government for their country's sake and their own. Seizing the young King in his bedchamber at Kinross, they carried him to Stirling Castle, whereupon the unpopular Anglophile lords, having lost possession of the sovereign, broke up and sought refuge in flight. [9]

Alexander showed his predilection for Stirling by laying out an extensive pleasure-ground, known as the New Park, and by setting in order the older royal chase, which apparently had suffered from neglect. [10] Just about this time, however, more serious affairs claimed attention. King Haakon of Norway in 1263 set sail with his Viking Armada in order to oppose Alexander's designs of annexing the western islands. The fury of the autumn winds and the opposition of the Scots at Largs broke the Norse King's power; but the devastation of the Lennox was sufficient warning that the invaders might carry their depredations further inland; consequently Stirling Castle was provided with a special garrison till King Haakon had withdrawn his shattered fleet from the Clyde. [11] This is the only instance in historical times of the stronghold's being prepared for defence against a foe that had come across the sea.

The last of the Celtic Kings of Scots was not to draw his final breath in the castle beloved by his line, where Alexander I. and William the Lion had laid themselves down to die. The third Alexander's fall from the cliff near King-

10

horn in 1286 was followed by years of grievous distress, in sad contrast to the flourishing days which had suddenly come to an end. Yet in the time of national prosperity, the King's own later years were clouded by misfortune. His Queen, the sister of Edward I., died unexpectedly in 1275, his daughter Margaret predeceased him, as did his two sons, Alexander and David, the latter of whom expired in Stirling Castle at the early age of ten. Four years after the King's fatal ride, his granddaughter, the Maid of Norway, passed away, her death giving rise to the disputed succession and the subsequent struggle with England.

Had this infant princess survived, she would have become the wife of the King of England's heir; and the Union of the Crowns would thus have taken place more than three hundred years before it actually occurred. The death of the Maid of Norway ruined the plans of Edward I.; he had now to devise a less straightforward scheme for bringing Scotland under his control.

Chapter Two - The War of Independence

The county of Stirling has aptly been called the "Battlefield of Scotland," for no less than six memorable conflicts have taken place in this district within historical times. During the wars with England, in the period of the Stewart sovereigns, the Borders and the neighbourhood of Edinburgh were the principal scenes of operations; but Stirling Castle was the centre of hostilities in the stirring days of Wallace and Bruce. Edinburgh, though an important fortress and town, was not the capital of the country at the time of the War of Independence. In later years, the armies of England did not need to advance any further than Lothian. The heart of Scotland lay south of the Firth of Forth; a blow struck there was felt throughout the kingdom. But in the beginning of the fourteenth century no fixed seat of government existed; and thus the chief aim of the leaders of both nations was to occupy the place of greatest strategic value. The strong position of Stirling Castle, near the head of the country's most important estuary, guarding the fords of the River Forth, and keeping watch over the passes leading to the Highlands, made the castle the focus of the military operations of both the English and the Scots. Seven times in half a century the veteran fortress changed hands.

When Edward I. agreed to act as arbiter in the case of the Scottish succession he startled the competitors by demanding their acknowledgment of his claim to be Lord Paramount of Scotland. The selfish disputants, each anxious to obtain the prize of even a vassal kingdom, and not being stirred with the patriotism which was to be born of the coming struggle, reluctantly consented to admit the English King's pretension, while the guardians of the realm apparently saw no way of avoiding civil war except by concurring in this base arrangement. It was agreed, therefore, in 1291, that Edward should have seisine of Scotland and its royal castles until two months after the award of his arbitrament; and in accordance with this compact a southerner, named Norman Darcy, was placed in command of Stirling Castle.

In November, 1292, judgment was given in favour of the feeble John Balliol, who almost immediately swore fealty to the English King and who was crowned soon afterwards at Scone. Weak though he was, however, the new King of Scots could not endure the oppressive exactions of his overlord. At first he obeyed when his suzerain summoned him to court, but soon he renounced his allegiance and opened negotiations with France, thus forming a friendship that developed into a close alliance to last till the reign of Queen Mary. Edward invaded Scotland with a powerful army to punish his perfidious vassal. The town of Berwick was mercilessly sacked, the Scots were defeated by Surrey at Dunbar, and the English monarch made a triumphal procession through Scotland, arriving at Stirling in the middle of June, 1296. So dispirited had John Balliol's subjects become that the castle garrison fled at the approach of the invading host, leaving only the porter to deliver the keys of the fortress to the English King. [12]

THE ABBEY CRAIG AND RIVER FORTH.

The rise of Wallace inspired the Scots with courage. They required a man of might to lead them and not a "Toom Tabard," or empty jacket, as they called their English-made King. It was a fearless band of patriots that was posted on the Abbey Craig on an autumn day of 1297, waiting to swoop down on the troops of Warenne and Cressingham. The English commanders made the mistake of attempting to cross the Forth by Stirling Bridge, thus playing into the hands of Wallace, whose spearmen rushed from the steep hillside and caught their foes in a trap. A great many of the garrison, including the constable, were slain or were drowned in this valley of death hardly more than half a mile from their fortress. [13]

After the defeat, Sir Marmaduke de Twenge endeavoured to hold Stirling Castle for King Edward, but, receiving no succour from the south, he was soon obliged to retire from his dangerous seat, leaving it to Wallace and the Scots. Falkirk, in the following year, avenged the battle of the bridge. Wallace, with a number of fugitives, fled to Stirling Castle, but realising the impossibility of holding the fortress against the English army, he dismantled it and withdrew. Edward pushed on to Stirling, where he rested for some days to recover from a kick from his horse, his men being employed in rebuilding the castle as a station for another English garrison.

Little more than a year elapsed, however, before the Scots laid siege to the fortress. The defenders appealed to their King for aid; but the winter had set in, and Edward could not induce his barons to advance into the heart of Scotland. The only course open to him, therefore, was to authorise the governor, John Sampson, to surrender. The garrison, accordingly, some ninety in number, delivered up the stronghold to the patriots, whose commander's name of Gilbert Malerbe seems unsuited to a leader of a band of Scots. [14] This same Gilbert proved faithless to the Scottish cause, and years afterwards he was hanged at Perth for treachery to King Robert the Bruce.

The custody of the perilous castle of Stirling was entrusted to the chivalrous knight, Sir William Oliphant. He must have almost daily expected his hour of trial to be at hand; but not until 1304 was the stronghold besieged by King Edward, for on two previous occasions when he journeyed past Stirling, the King was not prepared to attack the strongest castle in Scotland. In that year, however, every effort was made to secure the fortress for England. Oliphant informed the King that he held the castle for Sir John de Soulis, one of the Scottish guardians, who was at this time resident in France, and that if Edward would grant him a truce to enable him to go abroad, he would bring back word from his superior.

But the King, furious at the stubborn opposition of the Scots, replied: "To no such terms will I agree; if he will not surrender the castle let him keep it against us at his peril." On receiving this answer the garrison felt that their only course of action was to hold out to the last extremity. The siege began on the 22nd of April, and for three months the gallant defenders withstood the attack of the most formidable artillery which the English King could command. Edward had written to the Prince of Wales urging him to strip the lead from the churches of Perth, Dunblane and other places—leaving only the altars covered—in order to provide weights for the military engines. [15] He commanded also the Sheriff of York to dispatch forty cross-bowmen and forty carpenters to Stirling, [16] while the governor of the Tower of London was required to send north all the ammunition that was under his care in that arsenal. [17] So anxious indeed was the King to secure the assistance of his most experienced soldiers, that he forbade his knights to participate in tournaments without his special permission. [18]

While the English battered the walls of the castle with stones and leaden balls, and threw the combustible known as Greek Fire to damage the engines and injure the men, the defenders kept up a constant shower of javelins and other missiles. The King himself was struck by a weapon that lodged in a joint of his armour, and once a large stone fell so near his horse that the animal took fright and fell with his royal master. At last the stronghold was rendered untenable, for the walls were broken down in many places and the food supply was exhausted; but before the starving survivors of the garrison were allowed to issue forth, Edward experimented on the long-suffering fort with his most formidable engine, the War-Wolf. The Queen and her ladies viewed this assault from an oriel window constructed for the purpose. [19]

The Scottish historians maintain that Edward broke his word to the defenders, but they seem to have surrendered unconditionally, not being in a position to make stipulations. William Oliphant, William de Dupplin, William de Ramsay, Ralph de Halliburton, Alan de Vipont, John Napier and others were led half-naked before His Majesty, who spared their lives, but put them in chains and sent them to various English prisons. The King entered into possession of the castle on July 24th, 1304.

All the Scottish fortresses were now in Edward's hands, and in the following year his arch-enemy, Wallace, was captured and put to death. But Scotland, though crushed, was by no means conquered, for just at this time rose Robert Bruce to kindle the almost extinguished sparks of patriotism into an unquenchable flame. Stirling Castle, however, remained for ten years in English keeping in charge of various constables. John Lovel was the first to take over the fortress, but he was succeeded next year by William Bisset, a Scot in the King of England's service. Another Scotsman was Philip Mowbray, who held the castle for Edward II. after all the other strongholds in the country, except Berwick and Bothwell, had been won for King Robert the Bruce. The English tenure ceased the day after the decisive Scottish victory at Bannockburn.

The great battle that established the freedom of Scotland was fought almost under Stirling rock. Indeed, to reach the castle itself was the object of the English invasion. The events leading up to the conflict are well known. In the spring of 1313, Edward Bruce, brother of King Robert, invested Stirling, but growing impatient with the long-protracted siege, he imprudently agreed to the one-sided bargain which Mowbray audaciously proposed. The compact was that the fortress should surrender if not relieved by June 24th, Saint John the Baptist's Day, in the following year. Edward Bruce's consent to this arrangement may have been given in the hope that it would terminate the war by bringing about a decisive pitched battle. Both nations, at any rate, prepared for the coming struggle; for it was clear that the duty of the English monarch was to succour his northern castle, while the Scottish King's task was to block the way of any relieving army.

On June 23rd, 1314, Edward II., with his vast feudal host, amounting, perhaps, to fifty thousand men, came in sight of Stirling Castle, but between him and his goal lay Bruce's Scottish troops, relying not upon their numbers but upon their valour and the skill of their commanders. The main body of the English army apparently kept to the low ground near the Forth, while the advanced guard marched on the higher land to the south, and encountered the Scots on the border of the New Park. Here Bruce slew de Bohun in single combat, while Sir Robert Clifford, with a troop of horse, pushed on to relieve the Castle of Stirling. Randolph, with a company of spearmen, intercepted this English force, and after a stubborn engagement drove them back on their own lines. King Robert's successful duel and the triumph of Randolph's men caused the whole of King Edward's advanced guard to retreat before the elated Scots. It was on the next day, the 24th of June, that the armies came fully into contact. The English had passed the night in the carse, which in those days, even in summer, was a marshy tract of country. Barbour, the author of *The Brus*, was told that the Stirling garrison assisted the movements of the Southrons by carrying doors and shutters from the castle, under cover of darkness, and laying them over the numerous pools.

STIRLING CASTLE FROM BANNOCKBURN.

The question of the exact site of the battle has provoked a good deal of dispute. Tradition favours the ground between the Borestone Hill and the burn, and this most likely was the scene of the skirmish that followed the death of de Bohun. The great conflict of the ensuing day, however, seems to have been fought out on the low land near the confluence of the Bannock and the Forth, where the English, hemmed in by the two streams, were unable to take advantage of their superiority in numbers. [20] The Lanercost chronicler mentions that he heard from an eye-witness that the English in the rear were unable to fight owing to the leading division being in the way, and that there was nothing they could do but take to flight.

Barbour states that after the battle the King of England fled to Stirling Castle, but was counselled by Mowbray to depart with all speed, as the place could no longer be held. There are people who find it impossible to believe this and another statement by the same writer to the effect that many fugitives sought refuge on the castle rock, for the most obvious way of retreat would be south-eastwards, across the Bannock. Great weight, however, must be given to Barbour's account, for the poet derived his information from men who had actually fought in those wars, and in many cases his testimony is corroborated by other records and documents. The *Scalacronica* makes Sir Giles de Argentine urge the King to flee to the castle. The author of that work, Sir Thomas Gray, no doubt acquired his knowledge from his father, who witnessed but did not take part in the battle, having been brought by Randolph to the Scottish camp after the engagement with Clifford. Most of the fugitives probably escaped across the Bannock, but doubtless some found their way to

15

the castle past the Scottish left flank; and it must be remembered that King Robert kept his men well in hand and would not allow them to begin the pursuit till the day was indisputably won, lest their foes, realising the strength of their own numbers, should make a successful rally. History furnishes other examples of portions of defeated armies retreating round and behind their conquerors. It is well known that after the Battle of Prestonpans, Sir John Cope's soldiers fled in all directions except towards the Firth of Forth.

Stirling Castle surrendered on the following day, and Sir Philip Mowbray transferred his allegiance to the King of Scots when he handed over the keys of the fortress. Bruce, in accordance with his policy of dismantling all strongholds that might harbour English garrisons, destroyed the fortifications, but in his later years he sometimes resided within its weakened walls.

Although the War of Independence is usually regarded as having been brought to a close at Bannockburn, it is more correct to consider the latter part of Bruce's reign as a break in the long-enduring struggle. After King Robert had been laid to rest, Edward Balliol saw his chance of winning his father's crown, and soon the King of England advanced the old claim put forward by his grandfather, The Hammer of the Scots. Balliol's victory at Dupplin in 1332 was followed a year later by the Battle of Halidon Hill, the English revenge of Bannockburn. Edward III. garrisoned the defenceless castle of Stirling in 1336, placing Sir Thomas de Rokeby in command. The work of renovation was straightway begun. New walls were at once constructed, two wells—one in the castle proper, the other in the nether bailey—were cleared out and deepened; [21] hall, pantry, kitchen, larder, etc., were all repaired, and men were employed in Gargunnock Wood in hewing down trees for the timber-work of the fortress. The Scots were not long in attacking the strengthened castle, but before the defenders were reduced to their last extremity, the King of England appeared upon the scene and immediately raised the siege. Wyntoun and Fordun tell of a Scottish knight named Keith, who, when attempting to scale the wall, lost his footing and was killed by falling on his spear. Quantities of provisions were thereafter sent to Sir Thomas de Rokeby, lest the Scots should again surround the rock and cut off his supplies. [22] These precautions were indeed necessary, for the patriots under Robert the Steward renewed the siege towards the end of 1341, but so well had the garrison been victualled that not until April of the following year was it compelled by hunger to capitulate. The English garrison consisted of Sir Thomas de Rokeby, Sir Hugh de Montgomery, fifty-seven esquires, ten watchmen and sixty-two archers. [23]

According to Froissart, cannon were employed during this investiture of Stirling. His statement is not substantiated by any other authority, but as he was in the habit of enquiring eagerly for details about the events of which he

THE PROSPECT OF STIRLING CASTLE.

From Engraving by Captain John Slezer, *circa* 1693.

wrote, and as he visited Scotland before the generation had passed away that had taken part in these wars, it is probable that his information is correct. This seems to have been the first occasion on which gunpowder was used in Scotland, for Barbour mentions that the town of Berwick was not provided with "gynis for crakkis" when the English laid siege to it in 1319, but he says that during the invasion of England in 1327 the Scots saw for the first time the mysterious "crakkis of wer."

No further attempts were made by King Edward to regain possession of Stirling Castle. His efforts to win the crown of France diverted his attention, and the Hundred Years' War had already broken out. No second Bannock-burn closed the latter portion of the War of Independence; such a triumph could not take place under so unpatriotic and degenerate a King as the son of the valiant Bruce. Yet Scotland wrestled through the storm, though not until the High Steward had succeeded his worthless uncle on the throne was the nation safe from the grasping hand of her more powerful neighbour.

Chapter Three - The Early Stewarts

On the death of David II. in 1371, the crown passed to Robert the Stew-ard, grandson of the Bruce, in accordance with the succession settlement made at the Parliament of 1318. The first of the Stewarts was past middle life when he mounted the Scottish throne, and although he had been a man of war in his youth, he longed to spend his later years in the enjoyment of re-pose. To some extent his desire was fulfilled, for the war with England—which continued in spite of a truce—was of a fitful nature and not a desper-ate struggle for freedom. The King's favourite seat was the Castle of Rothe-say, but he occasionally made Stirling his place of residence, finding it a con-venient resting-place between Bute and St. Andrews or Perth.

For a number of years Sir Robert Erskine had been keeper of Stirling Cas-tle, and in 1373 the sovereign's son Robert, Earl of Menteith and Fife, and afterwards Duke of Albany, was appointed to fill the office. For the mainte-nance of this important position the Earl received an annual grant of four-teen chalders of corn and twelve chalders of oatmeal from the lands of Both-kennar, as well as an income of two hundred merks from the Lord Chamber-lain of Scotland. [24] The money was to be levied from the crown lands and from feudal dues in the shire of Stirling; but this arrangement did not long hold good, as a few years afterwards the fee was paid from the Treasury. It was in the power of the keeper to appoint and dismiss the constable and jan-itors of the castle. The Earl of Fife did not neglect the duties of his office, for the Exchequer Rolls bear witness to much strengthening and repairing of the fortress; alterations doubtless rendered necessary by the use of gunpowder in war. If Froissart is to be trusted, these fortifications served their purpose well, as he declares that an unsuccessful attack was made upon the castle by the soldiers of Richard II. Other chroniclers, however, do not refer to Stirling in connection with the invasion of 1385; they imply that the English army advanced little further than Edinburgh, being compelled by the wasted condition of the country to retreat across the Border.

Robert II. was succeeded in 1390 by his eldest son John, Earl of Carrick, who chose to reign as Robert III., John being considered an unlucky name for kings. Even less a man of action than his father, he allowed his ambitious brother, whom he created Duke of Albany, to manage the chief affairs of state. A younger brother, the Earl of Buchan, usually called the "Wolf of Badenoch," lived like an independent sovereign in the Highlands, and with his sons committed depredations on the low-lying districts of Angus and Moray. These unruly sons were taken captive, however, and sent to prison in Stirling Castle, where they were under the eye of the keeper, their uncle, Robert of Albany.

The age of chivalry had hardly yet passed its zenith. It was still the delight of gentlemen to travel from Court to Court displaying their prowess in feats of arms. In 1384 a number of French knights landed in Scotland desirous of finding adventures in the Border wars, as their country afforded no field for their activities since peace had been made with England. Otterburn, a few years later, was more a chivalric tournament *à outrance* than a serious battle between the armies of two hostile nations. A tournament for passages of arms was arranged to take place at Stirling in 1398. The principal combatants were to be Sir Robert Morley, a renowned English knight, and Sir James Douglas of Strabrock. The barriers were prepared and all was in readiness, when it was announced that the English champion, in a tilting match with a Scot named Thomas Traill, had suffered an unexpected defeat, and in consequence of the disgrace to his knighthood had taken to his bed and died.

A strange and ghost-like figure appeared in Scotland in the reign of Robert III. This was a half-crazed individual, called Thomas Warde of Trumpington, who bore a striking resemblance to King Richard II. He had been found in the castle of the Lord of the Isles at Islay, and was brought forward as a person likely to be of advantage in times of trouble with England. The uncertainty regarding Richard's end led many on both sides of the Border to believe that the King had escaped from Pontefract Castle; but the simpleton at the Scottish Court denied that he was Richard, while a report was spread that the deposed English monarch was hiding in the mountains of Wales. At all events a so-called King of England, known in history as the "Mammet" or false King, was maintained for political purposes in Stirling Castle, where he died in 1419, without having ventured to cross the Border to fight for the English crown.

During the regencies of Robert of Albany and his son Murdoch, who succeeded to the dukedom and to the office of keeper of Stirling Castle, carpenters and masons were employed from time to time in repairing and improving the fortress. The Chapel was to a large extent rebuilt in 1412, the year that saw the erection of the Chapel of Linlithgow Palace. Duke Robert died in Stirling Castle in 1420, and four years later James I. returned to his native country after eighteen winters of captivity in England.

The author of *The Kingis Quair* was an eminent poet, an accomplished knight, a constitutional monarch and a man of iron will. He was determined to strengthen the power of the Crown, not for his own selfish ends, but for the purpose of bringing the country into order. Unfortunately, however, he carried out his policy with haste and with merciless severity. Stirling was made the scene of James's relentless harshness only a year after his coronation at Scone. The King came to reside in the castle, and held a court on the 24th of May, 1425, at which he presided crowned and in his robes of state. A jury consisting of twenty-one barons, among whom were the Earls of Douglas, March and Angus, condemned Walter Stewart, Albany's eldest son, on a charge of robbery. The unfortunate man was promptly executed on the Heading Hill of Stirling. Next day the same jury, evidently acting in accordance with the King's desires, pronounced Duke Murdoch and another son guilty, although the crimes for which they suffered have not been brought to light. Doubtless James believed that the lawless state in which he found his kingdom was due to the misgovernment of the Albanys, and he may have thought that the Regents did not sufficiently exert themselves to procure for him an earlier release. The prospect of acquiring the estates of his kinsmen may also have influenced James. At any rate, the blood-stained Heading Hill witnessed the deaths of the father and the brother of its previous sufferer, as well as that of Albany's father-in-law, the aged Earl of Lennox. Sir John Kennedy, a nephew of the King, was, a few years later, imprisoned in Stirling Castle. [25]

It is little wonder that the pitiless policy of James stirred up feelings of revenge amongst the nobles. His relatives were not the only prominent persons who felt their sovereign's severity. Sir Robert Graham, who had once been imprisoned by the King, and whose nephew had been deprived of the Earldom of Strathearn, resolved to rid Scotland of her rigorous ruler. The assassination took place at Perth; but Graham was captured and brought to Stirling, where he was cruelly tortured to death. He felt sure he would be looked upon as a national deliverer; but neither his own contemporaries nor later generations so considered him, for the Poet-King, in spite of his heartless repressive measures, has always been a popular hero in Scotland.

The boy King, James II., was crowned in Holyrood Abbey, and some time afterwards was brought by the Queen-Mother to Stirling Castle, which was at that time in the charge of Sir Alexander Livingstone of Callendar. The marriage of the Queen in 1439 to Sir James Stewart, the Black Knight of Lorne, gave Livingstone a pretext for taking over the guardianship of the royal child. Compelling Queen Jane to keep within the walls of her own chamber, he threw her husband and his brother into prison; after which an irregular Parliament acknowledged his right to the custody of the King. At the same time, the Queen made over to Livingstone her right to the tenure of Stirling Castle.

Sir William Crichton, the Chancellor, however, envious of his rival's power, determined to take possession of young James. Accompanied by a troop of horsemen, he secretly left Edinburgh with the intention of kidnapping the King as he took his exercise in the Royal Park. The enterprise was successful; for early one morning the boy was surrounded by a body of armed men, and was straightway carried to Edinburgh Castle, of which fortress Crichton was governor.

This James of the Fiery Face—so called because of a dark red mark on his cheek—made Stirling Castle a dower-house for his Queen, Mary, daughter of the Duke of Gueldres. In 1449, the year of the King's marriage, a knightly tournament was held in the level ground to the south of the castle, the combatants being two Burgundian knights, Jacques and Simon de Lalain, with a squire called Meriadet, and three Scottish champions, James, brother to the Earl of Douglas, James, brother to Douglas of Lochleven, and John Ross of Halket. The six warriors were entertained by the King before the jousting took place,

THE DOUGLAS WINDOW.

and on the appointed day they appeared before James as he sat in his pavilion, and received from him the order of knighthood. The nobles of Scotland flocked to Stirling to witness the encounter, which was to be fought to the death or until the King should command the combatants to desist.

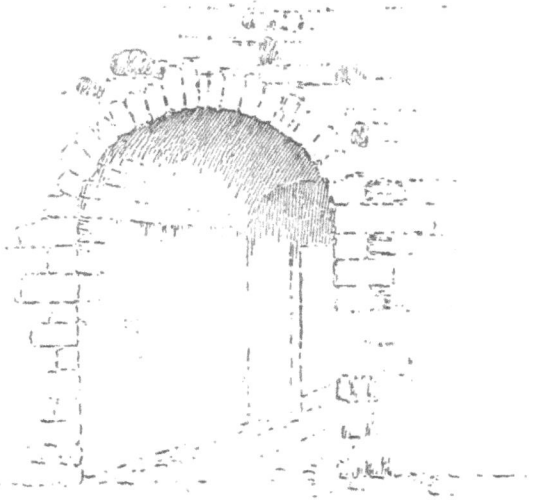

21

After trumpets had been sounded and proclamations had been made, the warriors eagerly advanced to the contest. The Earl of Douglas's brother and Jacques de Lalain managed to disarm each other and so continued the fight by wrestling; Simon de Lalain's coolness of head enabled him eventually to obtain a slight advantage over the Laird of Halket; the Lochleven Douglas, though twice struck to the ground, persistently returned to the attack, but was hardly able to hold his own with the skilful Meriadet. When at last the King threw down his truncheon as a signal for the conflict to cease, the marshals of the field laid hold of the struggling champions and compelled them to disengage. Neither side could claim a decisive victory, though the advantage, on the whole, lay with the foreign knights. King James, however, praised the valour of each individual, and before the Burgundians returned to their own country, he entertained them sumptuously in Stirling Castle and loaded them with gifts.

If the feats of arms of the Douglases brought honour to the chivalry of Scotland, their insatiable ambition was a danger to the King and gave rise to the evils of civil war. Earl William's vast estates—increased by his marriage with the Fair Maid of Galloway—and his descent from King Robert II., led him to consider himself the equal of his sovereign, and tempted him to plot against the throne. James was at this time doing his utmost to make himself master in his own realm. He had already imprisoned Sir Alexander Livingstone and his sons, and had given to Sir William Crichton the keepership of Stirling Castle. The conspiracy of Douglas is a somewhat mysterious affair. His loyalty had been questioned, but in the beginning of 1452 he seems to have been on friendly footing with James. There was, however, a rumour that Earl William had formed a plan of rebellion in conjunction with the Earl of Ross and the Tiger Earl of Crawford. Hoping to persuade his mighty subject to abandon his treasonable designs, James invited him to visit Stirling Castle and sent him a letter of safe-conduct under the privy seal. Douglas accordingly presented himself to his sovereign, and as the interview was marked by mutual goodwill, the Earl was asked to dine and sup with the King on the following day. At their second meeting all went well till after the evening meal, when James ventured to broach the subject of the Ross and Crawford league. Douglas's obstinate refusal to break the band roused the royal wrath to such a pitch, that, exclaiming, "False traitor, if you will not I shall," the King twice plunged his knife into Earl William's body. Sir Patrick Gray, Sir Alexander Boyd, Stewart of Darnley and other courtiers soon dispatched the helpless noble, and having finished the work of butchery, rudely flung the corpse out of the window.

James's hasty deed was a blunder as well as a crime. He had great provocation, it is true, but even if he had not pledged his word that Douglas should be safe, he had no right to slay him without a fair trial. His act gave excuse to the slaughtered man's family to rise against their King, and thus he fomented the civil strife which he was so anxious to suppress. After the lapse of several weeks, James, the new Earl—he that had fought in the tournament with the knights of Burgundy—accompanied by his brother, the Earl of Ormond, and by Lord Hamilton, rode to Stirling with six hundred men to defy the King of Scots. After exhibiting in public the letter of safe-conduct and dragging it at a horse's tail through the principal streets, they showed their open disregard for their sovereign by plundering and burning the town. James's throne was at this time in considerable danger. Public sympathy was to some extent with the Douglases. A three years' struggle ensued, in which the King gradually strengthened his position, till the Douglases were crushed in 1455 at the battle of Arkinholm in Eskdale.

Stirling Castle was the birthplace of James II.'s son and successor in 1451. Eight years later the bursting of a cannon killed the father at Roxburgh, so that Scotland had again the misfortune to be under a minor King. Many of James III.'s early days were spent in royal Snowdon, the residence that soon became his favourite dwelling-place. Lindsay of Pitscottie remarks that "he took such pleasure to dwell there that he left all other castles and towns in Scotland, because he thought it most pleasantest dwelling there." When Margaret of Denmark, in 1469, married James III., she received the castle as a portion of her dower, and within its gates she breathed her last, two years before the death of her husband. It was at Stirling that James entertained his low-born favourites: Cochrane, the architect; Rogers, the musician; Andrews, the astrologer; Hommyl, the tailor; and others. From the towers of the fortress he studied the stars, anxious to know what the future held in store. A King devoted to music, arts and science, but disliking war and manly sports, was not a monarch suited to fifteenth century Scotland. James's brothers, Albany and Mar, would have made better rulers. It was long, however, before the smouldering discontent in the country burst into the fire of rebellion.

King James III. wrought many improvements at the castle. The Parliament Hall, which is still in existence, dates from his reign, and was probably designed by Cochrane. A new chapel was built at this time, and the King intended to make it a collegiate church, but its erection to that dignity did not take place till his son had been some years upon the throne. His interest in the welfare of the Chapel Royal was the occasion, though not the main cause of James's fall. He endeavoured to attach to it the revenues of Coldingham Priory, a religious house in the Merse, in the country of the Homes and Hepburns. Patrick and James Home, however, had already annexed the funds, which they considered were their due, and they determined to resist an encroachment on their rights. The alliance of the Hepburns with the Homes was the beginning of the insurrection that soon spread far and wide, involving among other lords the Earls of Angus and Argyll.

The King at once made preparations for the struggle. Having placed his son, the Duke of Rothesay, in Stirling Castle, under the care of Shaw of Sauchie, he journeyed to the north to raise the subjects whom he knew to be loyally disposed. During the King's absence the rebels secured the person of the heir-apparent, who was treacherously handed over by the fickle Shaw. James returned south with a large army to meet the insurgents at Blackness, where a skirmish and a subsequent pacification took place. Hostilities, however, broke out afresh. The King was refused admittance to Stirling Castle, and the rebel army was advancing from Falkirk. A battle called Sauchieburn or the Field of Stirling was fought near Bannockburn, on June 11th, 1488, in which the charges of the Border spears eventually drove the King's Highlanders from the field, and during the flight the unhappy monarch was overtaken and slain. His body was buried near the High Altar in the Abbey of Cambuskenneth, where his Queen Consort, Margaret of Denmark, had not long before been interred. The engagement at Sauchieburn is interesting as being the only occasion in Scottish history in which Highlanders and Borderers were opponents on the field of battle.

The rebel Duke of Rothesay, a lad in his sixteenth year, mounted the throne as King James IV. in his luckless father's room. Soon after his accession he visited Stirling Castle and there expressed contrition for his part in the late insurrection, but a few months later he gave the keeping of the fortress to the traitor, Shaw of Sauchie. All through his later life, however, James IV. felt remorse for his conduct towards his father, and he often retired from Holyrood to Stirling when fits of depression were upon him.

Yet, subject as he was to sudden changes of mood, James could turn quickly from fasting and praying to the pleasures of society and the excitement of the chase; indeed, his reign was probably the gayest period in Stirling Castle's history. The King's genial nature broke through the gloom of remorse and gave mirth and gladness to a brilliant Court. The affairs of state having been transacted, the days were often spent in hawking expeditions, or in tilting matches, in which foreign knights sometimes took part, while the evenings were passed in playing cards and in listening to performances given by the royal minstrels on various musical instruments. James's expeditions in pursuit of the deer were not confined to the Royal Park. He often set out with a large retinue from Stirling to enjoy his sport in the neighbouring Highlands, and on those occasions tents were taken for the accommodation of the King and his nobles. [26] After one of those excursions, more than three hundred men were paid for having assisted James and his suite in their hunting in the forest of Glenartney. [27]

In 1496 the King's mistress, Margaret, daughter of John, Lord Drummond, resided for some months in Stirling Castle before being sent to Linlithgow. [28] James seems to have wished to have married this lady, but many of the leading nobles envied the power of the Drummonds, and the King saw what trouble would arise if he were to raise another member of the family to the throne; for David II. and Robert III. had both wedded daughters of that house. In 1502 Margaret and her two sisters fell suddenly ill, and died at Drummond Castle, but whether poison was administered at the instigation of envious nobles or not has never been ascertained. The three sisters were interred in Dunblane Cathedral, where, at the King's command, masses were said regularly for the welfare of Margaret's soul.

Great improvements were carried out both within and without the castle during the reign of James IV. The main gateway, much of which is still standing, was erected in the first decade of the sixteenth century. Other buildings were enlarged during the same period, while plasterers, painters, glaziers and wrights were in almost constant employment. Towards the end of the fifteenth century part of the low ground below the castle rock was converted into a garden, which soon was stocked with vines and fruit trees, as well as flowers and vegetables. In the June of 1508 the gardener of Stirling travelled twice to Holyrood with strawberries for the King.

James IV. was often at Stirling when ambassadors and other foreign visitors sought his presence, but the most famous alien who was received within the castle was the impostor, Perkin Warbeck. He arrived in Scotland in 1495, and was welcomed with great magnificence at Court as the son of Edward IV. The nobles, like their sovereign, received him with favour, Huntly actually, at James's request, bestowing the hand of his daughter upon him. A pension of £1200 a year was given to the princely visitor, whose clever acting completely deceived the generous King of Scots. James made war on England, mainly for Perkin's sake, in 1496 and the following year, but the impostor and the King of Scots eventually became estranged, and Warbeck set sail from Ayr in July, 1497.

The King carried out his father's wish regarding the raising of the Chapel Royal to the position of a collegiate church. In 1503 Parliament confirmed the appropriation of the rents of various lands and churches in the King's patronage for the support of the increased staff of clergy in the castle. Next year Pope Julius II. appointed the Bishop of Whithorn or Galloway Dean of the Chapel Royal, thus uniting the new collegiate church with the southern See of St. Ninian.

The clans of the west had troubled James IV. for many years, but before the end of his reign the defiant chiefs were subdued. The turbulent West Highlander, Donald Dubh, son of Angus of the Isles, having been captured by the Earl of Huntly, was imprisoned in Stirling Castle in 1506, before being removed to Edinburgh. He was probably one of the "Erschmen" mentioned in the Lord High Treasurer's Accounts as having been conducted by Andrew Aytoun "fra Striviling to Edinburgh," although the payment for clothes provided for Donald seems to have been long in reaching Aytoun's hands.

In 1507 an experiment, more foolish than interesting, was made at Stirling Castle in the presence of James IV. and his nobles. John Damian, a foreigner, known as the French Leech, had wormed his way by various arts into the King's favour. The alchemical investigations which he carried on at Stirling and elsewhere led James to reward his labours by appointing him Abbot of Tungland, in Galloway. Feeling that he was losing his place in the royal favour, however, Damian determined to reinstate himself by means of a hazardous enterprise. Announcing that with a pair of wings of his own making he would fly from the battlements of Stirling Castle and be in France before the King's ambassadors, he convoked a large assembly to witness his bold adventure. He sprang into the air, but fell at once to the ground, and was fortunate in escaping with no greater injury than the fracture of a leg. The jeers of the disappointed multitude caused the Abbot more pain than did the broken limb; but the King, ever fascinated by the foreigner's fatuous practices, received him again at Court. This incident is the subject of Dunbar's satirical poem called the "Ballad of the Fenzeit Freir of Tungland."

The brightness of the Court at Stirling was clouded by the shadow of approaching Flodden. Revels were interrupted by visits of ambassadors; the King was unable to cast care aside. Nicholas West, the envoy of Henry VIII., held several interviews with James in the castle in April, 1513. West did his utmost to induce the Scottish monarch to abandon the league with France. He was unwilling to leave James without extracting a promise that no invasion of England would take place when Henry crossed the Channel. The King of Scots stood firm, however, and would not agree to desert his old ally, so the disappointed and angry ambassador departed from Scotland, hating the people and being hated in return. Not many months later James lay dead on Flodden Field, and the nation suffered a blow from which it did not completely recover until its existence as a separate state had ceased.

Chapter Four - James V. and Mary

James V. in an especial sense belongs to Stirling Castle. True, Linlithgow was his birthplace, but he was brought at a tender age to Stirling, and although much of his early life was spent in Edinburgh Castle, he seems to have regarded ancient Snowdon as his favourite place of residence. It was usually from Stirling that James travelled in disguise to make himself acquainted with the habits of his people and to hear the complaints of his peasant subjects. The name "Gudeman o' Ballengeich," by which he chose to be called on those occasions, was a designation taken from a hollow or pass that separates the Gowan Hills from the castle rock of Stirling.

To this stronghold, which was her dower-house, Queen Margaret retired with her infant son after the battle of Flodden. Here in April, 1514, was born Alexander, Duke of Ross, James IV.'s posthumous son, a child that died in the castle of his birth less than two years later. When the Queen-Mother took the impolitic step of marrying the powerful young Earl of Angus in August, 1514, she made almost inevitable the loss of her position as Regent and as guardian of her sons. The Duke of Albany was summoned from France to rule in the land of his fathers, and although Margaret and her brother, King Henry of England, did all in their power to prevent his arrival, he landed in Scotland in 1515. Directly after his elevation to the Regency, Albany sent commissioners to Stirling for the purpose of compelling the Queen to deliver up her sons. Margaret met the nobles in the gateway of the castle; her hand was clasped in that of the young King, while a nurse stood behind bearing the infant Duke of Ross. The Queen commanded the intruders to halt until they should explain the nature of their mission. On hearing that they came to take over the custody of her sons, Margaret ordered the warder to drop the portcullis, and from behind its bars she delivered a speech justifying her conduct in refusing to surrender the castle. It is pleasant to record this dramatic incident in the life of James IV.'s widow, for the bold Tudor spirit displayed on this occasion shows that the character of the Queen-Mother was not entirely ignoble.

The defiance of his authority brought Albany with an armed force from Edinburgh. The Queen, therefore, realising the hopelessness of the situation, led the boy King to the gate, and made him with his own hands deliver the keys of the castle to the Duke. The Regent garrisoned the fortress with one

JAMES IV.'S GATEWAY (WHERE MARGARET TUDOR DEFIED THE COMMISSIONERS).

hundred and forty men, and gave the charge of it, with the custody of the princes, to the Earl Marischal and Lords Fleming and Borthwick. [29] Queen Margaret, after a brief stay in Edinburgh, returned to her native land, but finding it impossible to relinquish Scottish politics, she recrossed the Border in 1517. Her most memorable residence in Stirling Castle after her reappearance was during the winter of 1522–3, when an attack of smallpox injured her beauty and nearly put an end to her inglorious career.

In 1522 the boy James V. was placed under the care of Lord Erskine, who at the same time received the appointment of keeper of Stirling Castle. Strict precautions were taken to prevent the young monarch from being seized and carried off like his great-grandfather, James II. Twenty footmen were commissioned to be the nightly watch, taking turn by fours to guard the door of the royal chamber; and when the King rode out to the park he was to be preceded by six or eight horsemen and accompanied by a bodyguard. Only in "right fair and soft weather" was James to be allowed to take his sport. [30]

The King was thought to be old enough in 1524 to do without Lord Erskine's guidance. Margaret, consequently, took her son from Stirling to Edinburgh, where the nobles acknowledged the lad as an independent sovereign. His enjoyment of freedom did not last long, however, for in 1525 the Earl of Angus asserted himself, and by obtaining possession of the person of the King ruled the country for several years in his own and the English monarch's interests. Two unsuccessful attempts were made to rescue James from the Douglases' guardianship, but in 1528 he escaped to Stirling Castle by night, most probably from Falkland, as Pitscottie has it, although some have thought that the flight must have been from Edinburgh. The ambitious family was now to suffer for its insolent treatment of the King. Sentence of forfeiture was passed on the leading members of the house, and although Angus was for some time able to set his sovereign at defiance, he was at length compelled to retire for safety to England.

Archibald of Kilspindie was a Douglas who suffered banishment when his kinsmen fell into disgrace. Tiring of an exile's life in England, however, he resolved to throw himself on James's clemency. In 1534, accordingly, he made his way to Stirling, where he waited in the Royal Park as the King was returning from the chase. The monarch recognised the powerful figure of his old acquaintance, but did not stop to favour him with so much as a look of acknowledgment. Kilspindie ran by the side of the King, keeping pace with the horse up the hill towards the castle, but when they came to the entrance James rode straight on, leaving the breathless Douglas at the gate. The unhappy man's desire to spend his remaining years in Scotland was not fulfilled, for the King first sent him to Leith with Robert Barton, and afterwards commanded him to cross the sea to France. [31]

As in the previous reign, a distinguished ambassador from Henry VIII. visited the Court at Stirling. The messenger on this occasion was Lord William Howard, whose purpose in 1536 was to induce the Scottish King to meet his royal uncle in England. James's excuses seemed to irritate the English envoy, whose audacity and plainness of speech amounted almost to discourtesy. The King, at any rate, warned by his Council, would not promise to accede to Henry's wish; for his capture or some such calamitous occurrence was an event to be expected from the treacherous Tudor monarch.

Mary of Guise, James's second wife, as she journeyed from Fife to Edinburgh soon after her landing at Crail, crossed the Forth at Stirling, and beheld for the first time the towers of the castle in which she was afterwards to spend so many days. At this date the building known as the Palace was probably not completed, but nearly a year later, in the spring of 1539, when James V. came with his jousting gear to Stirling, he and his Consort may have lodged in the Renaissance addition, although it was still unfinished in 1541. The daughter of the first Duke of Guise took kindly to her adopted country and its people, and although in the years of her Regency, while Mary, her child, was in France, she underestimated the strength of the Reformation movement, and ruled mainly in the interests of her ambitious brothers, she nevertheless became a Scotswoman in sympathy, and learned to converse in the northern tongue as fluently as in French.

It was in James V.'s reign that the Reformation movement made itself manifest in Scotland. The King, not without hesitation, kept true to the Church of Rome, but his subjects were becoming increasingly dissatisfied with the ecclesiastical situation. Amongst the clergy themselves heretical doctrines were rapidly finding favour. Towards the close of James's life a Friar named Kyllour, or Keillor, set forth Christ's Crucifixion in the form of a play, and attracted large crowds at Stirling. One Good Friday morning the King was present at a performance held not far from the castle, and although the Friar's earnestness roused the wrath of the greater part of the audience against the bishops, and provoked at the same time the indignation of such priests as were present, James retired to his palace at the end of the display without showing whether his sympathies lay on the side of Friar Keillor or on that of the orthodox clergy. [32]

Many tales of James V.'s adventures in disguise must at one time have been current in the neighbourhood of Stirling, but unfortunately most of them have passed beyond recall. One story concerning the Gudeman of Ballengeich runs, however, as follows: Once when the Court was in residence at Stirling Buchanan of Arnprior commanded a carrier, who was journeying from the Lennox with commodities for the royal household, to leave him the entire load, for which a just price would be given. On the servant's refusing to obey this order Buchanan boldly took possession of the goods, telling the carrier that James might be King in Scotland but that Arnprior was King in Kippen. A day or two later His Majesty rode with one or two attendants to Buchanan's house in Kippen. James was refused admittance by a tall man bearing a battleaxe, who announced that the laird was at dinner, and would not be disturbed at his meal. A second time the disguised monarch demanded access to the house, and again he was denied entrance, but at length he persuaded the porter to carry in a message to the effect that the Gudeman o' Ballengeich was desirous of an interview with the King of Kippen. Arnprior at once guessed the truth, and coming out humbly to the King, begged him to enter and grace his subject's board. So well was James entertained that, before returning home, he requested Buchanan to take in future such provision as he should need from any royal carrier passing his door; also he invited the King of Kippen to return the unexpected visit by riding to Stirling Castle to see his neighbour, the King of Scots.

A few days before the death of James at Falkland his daughter Mary was born at Linlithgow in December, 1542. The Earl of Arran was appointed Governor of the realm; but in July, 1543, his rival, Cardinal Beaton, rode from Stirling with the Earls of Lennox, Argyll and Huntly, at the head of several thousand men, in order to secure the person of the Queen. Arran, reckoning the troops at his disposal insufficient to enable him to frustrate their designs, sent messengers to treat for peace, and allowed the infant Mary and her mother to be carried to Stirling Castle. The two Queens were placed in the charge of four nobles, the chief of whom was John, Lord Erskine, the constable of the fortress. On the 9th of September the young Queen of Scots was crowned in the castle, the Earls of Arran and Lennox taking part in the ceremony "with such solemnity," wrote Sadler, the English envoy, "as they do use in this country, which is not very costly." The solemnity, however, was costly enough to make the unconscious child a crowned Queen, and to give her a high position among European princes, also to stir up strife among the nations and to lead to the grim tragedy of Fotheringay Castle.

THE PASS OF BALLENGEICH.

For the next four years—save for a short time at Dunkeld during Hertford's expedition—the little Queen was carefully guarded in Stirling: a fortress further than Edinburgh from the greedy hand of Henry VIII. The English monarch had set his heart on wedding his son to Mary of Scotland, but he alienated the people of the northern kingdom by trying to coerce them into submission to his will. During these years the Queen-Mother at the castle kept in touch with the politics of the day. Here she received the joyful news of the Scottish victory of Ancrum Moor in 1545. Later she welcomed Lorges de Montgomery, who came with money and soldiers from France. In September, 1547, Arran rode in haste to the castle bearing the depressing tidings of the defeat and slaughter at Pinkie Cleuch. After this disaster even Stirling Castle was considered hardly a safe enough abode for the youthful sovereign of Scotland, so without delay she was conveyed to Inchmahome, an island priory in the Lake of Menteith. When the immediate danger was past the precious royal child was carried back to Stirling, before being removed to the fortress of Dumbarton, whence a few months later she set sail for the friendly realm of France. After her daughter's departure from Scotland Mary of Guise was often at Stirling, but she did not survive to welcome the young Queen home when she returned a girl widow in 1561. The battery at the south-east corner of the castle, overlooking Ballengeich, is known as the Spur or French Battery, the latter name recalling foreign workmen of Mary of Guise, who caused this fortification to be made at the time of the French occupation of Stirling during the religious dissension called the Wars of the Congregation.

After her return to the land of her fathers Queen Mary made Holyrood her principal seat. She sometimes, however, removed to the castle that had been the home of her early youth, finding it a useful halting-place on her journeys to and from the north. In September, 1561, she narrowly escaped being burnt in the Palace. One night as she slept the candle which had been left alight set fire to the curtains of her bed, and although the Queen was rescued from the flames, she was almost overpowered by the smoke. An old prophecy that a queen should be burnt at Stirling came near to being fulfilled. [33] Mary's short stay in the castle at this time was marked by another disturbance. On her chaplains' attempting to sing High Mass, her half-brother, Lord James, and the Earl of Argyll, in their zeal for the Protestant cause, attacked the priests and singers with such fury that blood was actually shed in the Chapel Royal. Some of those who witnessed the scuffle regarded it as an amusing entertainment; others, however, took it more to heart, and gave way to tears instead of laughter. [34]

The Queen's visit to Stirling in 1565 was of longer duration than usual. The cause of her protracted sojourn was the illness of Henry Stewart, Lord Darnley, to whom at this time she was passionately attached. This young Anglo-Scottish nobleman had recently come from Elizabeth's Court, and was confined to bed in Stirling Castle with an illness which developed into measles. [35] Throughout the months of April and May the Queen kept watch by the bedside of her lover, refusing to travel until he had recovered, and paying no heed to the danger of infection.

The royal marriage was celebrated at Holyrood in July, 1565, and in June of the following year Prince James was born in Edinburgh Castle. Two months later the infant heir was removed for greater safety to Stirling, the fortress that had sheltered his mother some twenty years before. Towards the end of the year Queen Mary followed her son to the castle, where elaborate preparations were being made for the infant's baptism and for the reception of the foreign ambassadors. Care was taken on this occasion that no Englishman should have reason to remark that "the solemnity was not very costly," for the Estates made a grant of twelve thousand pounds Scots to meet the expenses of the visitors' entertainment. The Prince's godmother, Queen Elizabeth, sent the Earl of Bedford with a massive golden font; the Count of

Brienne, representing Charles IX. of France, brought a pair of earrings and a necklace to the Queen; Morette, the Duke of Savoy's ambassador, who arrived too late for the ceremony, presented to Mary a handsome jewelled fan. On the late afternoon of the 17th of December, 1566, the six months old child was baptised in the Chapel Royal. Barons and gentlemen bearing torches lined the way from the nursery to the Chapel door, where the Prince was received by the Archbishop of St. Andrews and the Bishops of Dunkeld, Dunblane and Ross. The christening service was performed according to the rites of the Church of Rome, although the ceremony of the spittle was omitted at the express command of the Queen. The child was given the names of James and Charles, the former in commemoration of his Scottish ancestors, the latter as a compliment to the Most Christian King of France. The Earl of Bedford and the Scottish Protestant Lords—including Bothwell, who had been appointed superintendent of arrangements—stood outside the building while the Romish service lasted; but the Countess of Argyll, although a Protestant, held the royal infant up to the font. At the conclusion of the ceremony the company adjourned to supper, the remainder of the evening being spent in dancing and music.

The festivities in connection with James's baptism were not confined to the christening day. On the 19th of December the Queen held a banquet in honour of her distinguished guests, and after the party had risen from the table a display of fireworks was given. Later in the evening Mary created her son Prince of Scotland, Duke of Rothesay, Earl of Carrick, Kyle and Cunningham, and Baron of Renfrew. [36] In spite of the appearance of gaiety, however, all was not well at Court. Darnley, although residing in the castle, refused to be present at the baptism of his son and at the social functions that followed. By this time the Queen and he were completely estranged. His own selfish and disgraceful conduct had caused her to regard him with loathing, and her increasing interest in Bothwell aroused her husband's jealousy and led to his sulky behaviour. The Queen made an effort to seem joyous to her guests, but her heart was all the time heavy with trouble: Du Croc, the French ambassador, found her weeping in her chamber, suffering both mental and bodily pain. [37]

Sir James Melville also has placed it on record that at this time of gaiety Mary was in deep distress. She was sad and pensive, he said, and she continually gave great sighs; but few of those who were with her at the castle were able to extend to her the sympathy she needed. Melville, however, seems to have been a person in whom the Queen could confide. One evening, shortly before the baptism, she took him by the hand and led him down to the Royal Park, where they could discuss the troubles of the state without being interrupted by the mockery of Court festivities. After humbly proffering his advice and endeavouring to lighten her burden of sorrow, he escorted her back to the castle through the steep streets of the town. [38]

A source of unpleasantness on the evening of the banquet was the masque arranged by the Frenchman, Bastien. A number of men dressed as satyrs, entered the hall as the meat was being served, and seizing the long tails with which they had been furnished, wagged them in front of the English guests. It was an ancient jest among the Scots that their southern neighbours had tails, so whether Bastien intended to give offence or not, the Englishmen present felt highly insulted. [39] The angry voices behind her back attracted the Queen's attention. Instantly perceiving the cause of the uproar, she rose from her seat and addressed the unruly company, and so with the assistance of the Earl of Bedford she succeeded in putting an end to the tumult.

Mary remained at Stirling after the ambassadors had gone, but in the dismal weather of the middle of January she departed with her son for the capital. [40] Two months afterwards the Prince was carried back to Stirling Castle by the Earls of Huntly and Argyll, and placed in the charge of John, Lord Erskine, by this time Earl of Mar. [41] Meanwhile Darnley had perished at Kirk-of-Field, and Bothwell was plotting for his marriage with the Queen. Shortly before the consummation of that union, Mary paid her last visit to Stirling. She came with the natural desire to see her son and possibly with the object of removing him from the castle. The child, however, remained in the faithful hands of Mar, and in a few days the Queen, on her homeward journey, was intercepted and carried off by Bothwell. The marriage was celebrated in Holyrood Palace in May, 1567; but the ambitious and unscrupulous nobleman, not satisfied with being the husband of his sovereign, sought to gain possession of the person of the Prince, in order, as Sir James Melville says, to "warrant him fra revenging of his father's death." Mar, however, distrusting the Queen and regarding Bothwell as a murderer, refused to allow the Prince of Scotland to pass into even his own mother's keeping.

The Stewarts were an unhappy race, but James V. and Mary had the saddest lives of all. He was gifted with a joyous nature and a genuine love of justice, and yet when only thirty years old he died of a broken heart. She was endowed with beauty, vivacity, generosity and courage, but these brought her sorrow, captivity and death. The national disaster at Flodden Field was to a great extent responsible for those unhappy reigns. The country was crippled by the heavy blow and was more at the mercy of the English Crown than in the days of the early Stewarts. This was especially the case in James V.'s time, for his weariness of life was chiefly due to despair of being able to combat Henry's schemes.

The defeat had another effect, however, which gave rise to the troubles of Mary's reign. Almost all the nobles of Scotland fell with their King in battle, leaving, in many cases, minors to succeed. Consequently, the government passed into the hands of the prelates, who were mostly, at this time, men of low moral character and of selfish worldly aims. Moreover, the Regent Albany, in order to avert civil strife, filled the wealthy benefices with members of influential families. Thus the clergy grew more and more corrupt, and a Reformation became a necessity. The revolution did not break out in James V.'s days, mainly on account of that monarch's alliance with France and his distrust of his English uncle; but it accomplished its work with greater thoroughness because of its postponement, and directly after the change had been wrought, Queen Mary returned to Scotland. Yet had Flodden and Pinkie not been lost, the Queen in all likelihood would not have been sent to France to be reared at the Court of Catharine de' Medici and trained by the fiercely orthodox Guises, and Scotland might have been ruled by a sovereign who had not been educated in a form of faith that had become obnoxious to the majority of her subjects.

Chapter Five - James VI

Once more a minor became sovereign of Scotland. Not, however, as in former cases, by the early death of the preceding monarch did the throne become vacant again, but by a deed of abdication which the helpless captive Queen was compelled to sign at Lochleven. On July 29th, 1567—a few days after the close of Mary's reign—the thirteen months old Prince of Scotland was crowned at Stirling as James VI. The Chapel at the castle on this occasion was not the scene of the function, the High or Parish Church being chosen as a suitable place for the ceremony. The child was anointed by the Protestant Bishop of Orkney, while the Earl of Atholl held the crown over the royal head. Morton and Home took the oath for the King that he would maintain the true religion, and after Knox had preached a sermon, the company returned to the castle, Mar carrying the infant monarch and Atholl bearing the crown.

For twelve years after his coronation young James resided in Stirling Castle under the care of the family of Mar. During almost the whole of that period the government of Scotland was carried on in the name of the King by four Regents in succession; and Stirling, being the sovereign's seat, figured conspicuously in the history of the time. In September, 1569, at a council held in the castle by the Regent Moray, Maitland of Lethington was accused by Thomas Crawford of having taken part in the murder of Darnley. His trial being fixed for December 21st, Lethington was placed in confinement in the fortress, but a few days later he was carried to Edinburgh, where he managed to escape from bondage by the instrumentality of Kirkcaldy of Grange. [42]

Less than two years later there was thrust into Stirling Castle another prominent member of Queen Mary's dwindling faction. This was John Hamilton, Archbishop of St. Andrews, the prelate who had taken the leading part at the Prince's baptism not many years before. He had been seized in Dumbarton Castle on the memorable night when the King's men scaled the rock, and had been brought without delay to his enemies' headquarters. Like Maitland of Lethington, he was charged with having been implicated in the murder of James's father, and his confinement in Stirling, like Lethington's, lasted for only one or two days. The Archbishop, moreover, was held to be guilty of having encouraged Bothwellhaugh to assassinate the Regent Moray, so after a hasty trial he was hanged at the market cross in April, 1571.

Stirling, being at this time the young King's home, was naturally the headquarters of his mother's opponents. Edinburgh, where the castle was held for the Queen by Sir William Kirkcaldy of Grange, was the principal seat of Mary's less powerful party. A plan was accordingly devised by the Laird of Grange that nearly succeeded in changing, for a time at least, the course of Scottish history. Knowing that the leaders of the opposite faction were gathered together for a meeting of Parliament, he resolved to surprise and capture Stirling, to seize all the prominent supporters of the King, and to obtain possession, if possible, of the royal child himself. Kirkcaldy was anxious to conduct the expedition in person, but, being persuaded by his followers not to run such a risk, he appointed the Earl of Huntly, Lord Claude Hamilton, Scott of Buccleuch and Ker of Fernihirst to undertake the enterprise.

On the evening of the 3rd of September, 1571, these chiefs, accompanied by three or four hundred men, rode out of Edinburgh and took the road to Jedburgh in order to deceive their enemies as to the object of their journey. In the gathering darkness they wheeled to the right and made their way swiftly to within a mile of Stirling, where they halted and left their horses. [43] One of the party, a native of the place, knowing of the existence of a secret passage, guided the raiders into the town at an early hour in the morning. There was not even the bark of a dog to give the citizens alarm; the burghers and nobles were aroused by the cries of "A Hamilton" and "God and the Queen." Houses were instantly broken into and most of the lords were captured with ease, but at Morton's lodging some fighting took place, resulting in the slaughter of two of the Earl's retainers. Morton, however, eventually gave himself up to the Laird of Buccleuch, the Regent Lennox surrendered to Spens of Wormiston, and the Earls of Glencairn and Eglinton also submitted themselves to the adventurers.

The Queen's party seemed to have triumphed completely, but their easily-won victory led to their defeat. The Borderers, unable to resist the temptation of plunder, rushed in all directions in search of booty, so that when the Earl of Mar sallied forth from the castle with a band of musketeers, a panic at once ensued. The citizens armed themselves and turned on their despoilers, while the castle soldiers kept up a fire from behind the walls of Mar's unfinished house. The raiders were demoralised and quickly took to flight, but rather than allow the Regent Lennox to be rescued, a man named Calder fired his pistol at the Earl. By throwing himself in front of his distinguished prisoner, Spens of Wormiston was shot, and the bullet passing through his body, mortally wounded Lennox. The dying Regent was conveyed to the castle, where in the evening he passed away. His death was deplored not only by his friends but by his foe, Kirkcaldy of Grange, who had desired the Raid of Stirling to be, if possible, a bloodless triumph. [44]

Little more than a year had elapsed when another Regent died in Stirling Castle. This was the King's hereditary keeper, John, Earl of Mar, who had been elected to govern the realm in the room of James's grandfather, Lennox. [45] The cares of state and the worries of the civil war seem to have been responsible for the Regent's premature decease, although the usual report of poisoning was given circulation at the time. Mar left the charge of the King and the castle to his brother, Alexander, Master of Erskine, for his son, the new Earl, a companion of James, was a boy not much older than the King.

The next governor, the Regent Morton, was in favour of the young sovereign's continuing his residence at Stirling. His education was meanwhile receiving attention from George Buchanan and Peter Young, the former a brilliant scholar and a strict disciplinarian, the latter too full of respect for the Lord's Anointed to oppose his pupil's wayward will. "My Lady Mar was wise and sharp," wrote Sir James Melville, "and held the King in great awe; and so did Mr. George Buchanan. Mr. Peter Young was gentler and was loath to offend the King at any time, and used himself warily, as a man that had mind of his own weal, by keeping of His Majesty's favour; but Mr. George was a Stoic philosopher, and looked not far before the hand."

In June, 1574, Killigrew, the English ambassador, visited Stirling Castle, and heard James translate into French a chapter, chosen at random, of a Latin version of the Bible; while to show that his accomplishments were not confined to intellectual pursuits, the King delighted the English envoy by an exhibition of dancing. [46] Weldon, in his oft-quoted description of James, writes: "His legs were very weak ... that he was not able to stand at seven years of age." [47] Weldon's unflattering portrait of the King is held by some to be a faithful representation; but the statement regarding James's physical weakness seems to be untrue, for if he could not stand at seven, he would surely be unable to give a display of dancing when exactly eight years of age. Later in the same year the two famous Melvilles—Andrew and his nephew James—were presented to their sovereign at Stirling. The younger man notes in his Diary that the boy monarch, on account of his strange and extraordinary gifts, was the sweetest sight in Europe that day. The writer goes on to say: "I heard him discourse, walking up and doun in the auld Lady Mar's hand, of knowledge and ignorance, to my great marvel and astonishment." [48]

James had companions at work and play in those schooldays at the castle. The young Earl of Mar, Lord Invertyle and others learnt their lessons with their King at Stirling. That Buchanan showed no favouritism in his dealings with his pupils will be seen by the following story, originally told by Invertyle: The Earl of Mar possessed a tame sparrow which the King was anxious to obtain.86 On the young nobleman's refusing to hand over the bird to his sovereign, a struggle between the two playmates ensued, ending in the death of the sparrow. Mar burst into tears at the loss of his pet, and Buchanan, being informed of the cause of the weeping, gave the King a box on the ear, and told him he was a true bird of the bloody nest of which he was come. [49]

That the stern preceptor was not devoid of humour the following anecdote will show. The young King's readiness to grant requests thoughtlessly was noted by Buchanan with distress. Determined to teach the boy a lesson, he requested him to sign two documents, the purport of one being to transfer the regal power to Buchanan for fifteen days. After asking one or two random questions, the sovereign willingly signed the papers without taking trouble to read their contents; and that same day the tutor acted the part of King to the astonishment of the courtiers and the utter amazement of James. At length Buchanan informed his pupil that he had temporarily resigned his crown, and as the King continued to appear bewildered, the document was produced. Before James had time to recover from his discomfiture, the tutor followed up his practical lesson by a discourse on the evils that are likely to accrue from the rashness and carelessness of kings. [50]

Buchanan's interest in education during the Stirling period of his life was not confined to the training and instruction of the monarch and his companions. He was appointed president of the commission which met in Stirling Castle to consider the question of a standard Latin grammar, as teachers had been complaining of the confusion arising from the various manuals in use throughout the country. The result of the proceedings was that Buchanan and two commissioners, Andrew Simson and James Carmichael, schoolmasters, undertook to produce a new book which was to supersede all the others. In due time the joint work of these eminent scholars appeared, but it never became established as the one and only grammar. [51]

The room still exists in the Keep of the castle where George Buchanan and Peter Young are believed to have discharged their pedagogic duties, and a terrace below is called the *Prince's Walk*, where James, it is said, was wont to take the air before returning to his studies. Doubtless the young King and his comrades romped on this narrow playground, but it owes its name more likely to James's son, Prince Henry, for the father was a crowned monarch before his education began, and the terrace is known not as the *King's* but as the *Prince's Walk*.

The regency of Morton was, on the whole, a time of peace, but his enemies were all the time planning his overthrow. The greater part of the nobility was hostile to the Regent; thus when the King, at the instigation of Argyll, and with the approval of Buchanan and Alexander Erskine, summoned a convention of peers to Stirling Castle in March, 1578, Morton felt compelled to send in his resignation. The clever Earl, however, soon found an opportunity of placing himself again in power. On the morning of the 26th of April, the young Earl of Mar, possibly acting on Morton's advice, called for the keys of the castle as though he intended to ride forth to hunt. Although the hour was about six o'clock the Master of Erskine was already astir, and meeting his nephew's followers at the gate, he called his servants to his assistance. After a scuffle, in which the Master's eldest son was so severely crushed that he died next day, the parties withdrew to the hall to discuss the situation. The proceedings resulted in the young Earl of Mar's being allowed to take over the charge of the King and the keeping of Stirling Castle. [52] It was also decreed that James was to remain in the castle, that no earl was to be received within the gates with more than two servants, no lord with more than one attendant, and no gentleman with any retainer at all. [53] The stirring events of that morning made such an impression on the youthful King, that for several nights his sleep was disturbed by visions of the fray.

Morton was not long in breaking through the decrees. Riding secretly by night from Edinburgh to Stirling, towards the end of May, he persuaded Mar to admit him and his followers into the royal castle. Once within the same building as the King, the Earl was now as powerful as before. He managed to arrange the formation of a new Council, with himself in the principal place, and he persuaded the King to order the Parliament, which

THE KEEP AND THE PRINCE'S WALK.

had been summoned to meet at Edinburgh, to assemble in the hall of Stirling Castle. The opponents of Morton, naturally objecting to the Estates being convened within the walls of a fortress, were determined not to appear without a protest, so they sent the Earl of Montrose and Lord Lindsay of the Byres to lay their remonstrances before the King. James opened the Parliament in person, and before any business was transacted, Lord Lindsay protested against its proceedings. Morton interrupted him and ordered him to sit down, but Lindsay disobeyed the command until it was repeated by the King. Later in the day the intrepid lord again arose to make objections, and this time also he was silenced by James, who, at Morton's prompting, declared that the Parliament was free and that those who loved him would think as he thought. [54]

Morton's recovery of power rendered civil war imminent. Argyll and Atholl raised the town of Edinburgh and were joined by the Borderers of Teviotdale and the Merse. Angus, on the other side, was preparing his forces at Stirling. The armies came within sight of each other near the town of Falkirk, and some skirmishing took place, but through the intervention of two leading ministers of the church and of Bowes, the English ambassador, an agreement was arrived at without any fighting taking place. The settlement left things much as they were, with the power in Morton's hands, but the Earl of Montrose and Lord Lindsay of the Byres were admitted into the Council.

Although not holding the title of regent, the Earl of Morton was now as powerful as ever he had been. His opponents felt themselves incapable of compelling him to deliver up their sovereign, and so secure did Morton consider his position and the King's to be, that on the 12th of June, 1579, James was allowed to leave the castle by the nether bailey gate at five o'clock in the morning, with his own domestics, and was permitted to remain in the Park until seven o'clock at night. This was the first occasion on which the King passed beyond the castle walls without the protection of an armed guard. [55]

Morton's day of triumph, however, was beginning to draw to a close. There arrived in Scotland a man from France, who quickly won the favour of King James, and who set himself to restore Queen Mary to the throne, to overthrow the Protestant religion in Scotland and to ruin the Earl of Morton. He was successful in only the last of these three enterprises. This remarkable person was Esmé Stewart, Lord of Aubigny in France, and nephew of the Regent Lennox. "He was a man of comely proportion, civil behaviour, redbearded, honest in conversation." [56] Recommended to James by the Guises, whose special agent he was, he arrived at Stirling in September, 1579, and was presented to the King in the hall of the castle. The artful schemer was not long in winning James's favour. Soon he received the wealthy Abbey of Arbroath, which had been in the possession of the Hamilton family, and about the same time he was made a privy-councillor and was given the Earldom of Lennox.

Esmé Stewart had not been many months at Court before a rumour was reported to the Earl of Mar to the effect that the half-foreign favourite and his partisans intended to remove the King to Dumbarton, and afterwards to convey him secretly to France. The night of the 10th of April, 1580, was believed to be the time arranged by the conspirators for carrying out their plan. The rumour, whether well-founded or not, gave rise to intense excitement in the castle. When the dreaded evening came round, Mar placed soldiers both within and without the King's apartment, and ordered them on no account to allow anyone to enter the room. Lennox, armed and supported by a guard of friends, prepared to defend himself in his own chamber, for he heard the threatening shouts in the courtyard and knew that his life was in danger.

The night passed away, however, without an attack being made upon Stirling, although in the morning the Earls of Argyll, Glencairn and Sutherland—

friends of Esmé Stewart, Lord Lennox—endeavoured without success to gain admittance to the castle. [57]

Lennox and another rising favourite, James Stewart, together worked for the hated Morton's fall, and as the King was completely in their hands and bore no love to the stern ex-regent, the Earl was condemned to death in 1581, for being "art and part" in the murder of Darnley. Yet not much more than a year after Morton's death, Lennox's ascendency came to an end. A number of nobles—Mar, Gowrie, Lindsay and others—seized the King at Ruthven Castle, near Perth, and virtually held him a prisoner, while Lennox was ordered to leave the country—a step which at last he reluctantly took. James was brought back to Stirling, and, although chafing at the restraint, was compelled to announce that he was a free King and that he desired to reside in the castle. But the Ruthven Raiders were unable to keep their sovereign for more than ten months in their hands. In June, 1583, a plot for the recovery of his freedom was formed, and he escaped from Falkland Palace to St. Andrews, where he threw himself into the castle.

Their inability to hold the King in their power was disastrous to the leaders of the Raid of Ruthven; consequently they lost little time in arranging a scheme to place themselves again in command. The Earl of Mar and the Master of Glamis had retired to the north of Ireland, but in the spring of 1584 they stealthily crossed the Channel, and on the 17th of April, with five hundred horse, they seized the Castle of Stirling. James at once raised an army in Edinburgh and marched to attack the rebels. No fighting of any sort took place, however, for the insurgent lords, taken aback by the King's swift action and disappointed in the support of their friends, fled towards the Border before the royal army appeared. The small garrison which they left to guard the fortress surrendered at once to the King. The constable and three of the men were hanged as a sign of the royal displeasure. [58] On the failure of the conspiracy, the Earl of Gowrie, who had come to be regarded with distrust by both parties, was tried at Stirling and executed almost beneath the walls of the castle.

In November, 1585, another Raid of Stirling occurred. The exiled lords who had forsaken the castle in the previous year, collected their forces in the south of Scotland, where they were joined by a number of the Border lairds. Proclaiming that they sought to save the King and the country from the evil rule of James Stewart, Earl of Arran, they advanced northwards with some nine hundred men and camped at St. Ninians on November 1st. Next morning at daybreak they crept into the town, like Buccleuch and Fernihirst fourteen years before, while Arran and Montrose, who had kept watch on the walls, immediately took to flight, the former seeking safety beyond the Bridge of Forth, the latter finding refuge in the castle with the King. Having captured the town with comparative ease, the lords proceeded to invest the fortress which they knew to be ill prepared for a siege. After sending messengers to treat with the invaders, James agreed to surrender, for his attempt to escape by bribing William Maxwell of Newark, who had charge of one of the postern doors, was discovered by the besiegers. The nobles entered the castle on the 4th of November, assuring their sovereign that they had acted from motives of loyalty, while he replied that words were unnecessary, as their weapons had spoken quite loudly enough. Differences were settled for the time, and James professed to be pleased with the change; Arran was banished for ever from the Court, and to Mar, who had forfeited his hereditary privilege, the custody of Stirling Castle was restored.

Too often in Scottish history the conduct of the barons towards the sovereign was insolent and disloyal; but there were occasions in which their coercive action was fraught with good to the country. The nobles who captured James VI. at Ruthven Castle and who besieged him in his own stronghold of Stirling, were actuated to some extent by selfish motives, but at the same time they realised that their measures were such as would confer real benefit upon the land. Yet although the weakness of the King in placing his trust in unpopular favourites justified the daring steps taken by the nobles, it is not a matter for wonder that in his later life the shout of "Treason" escaped from James's lips whenever an unexpected incident occurred.

James VI. married Anne, second daughter of Frederick II. of Denmark, in 1589, and Stirling Castle was chosen to be the birthplace of their eldest son, who was born in February, 1594. For the Prince's baptism great preparations were made, including the hasty reconstruction of the Chapel, for James was always anxious to impress his visitors with the dignity of the Scottish Court. The foreign representatives arrived at Stirling before the end of August, and on the 30th of that month the christening service was held. [59] The Prince was carried to the Chapel by Elizabeth's representative, the Earl of Sussex, who walked under a canopy supported by the Lairds of Cessford, Buccleuch, Dudhope and Traquair; and in the procession Lord Hume carried the ducal crown, Lord Seton bore the basin and Lord Livingstone the towel. The chief officiating clergyman was David Cunningham, Bishop of Aberdeen, who at the King's command named the royal infant Frederick Henry, and thereafter addressed the congregation in Latin. At the conclusion of the service the company retired to the Prince's chamber, where James created his child a knight and bestowed on him the usual titles belonging to the eldest son of the King. After a number of less important knights had been made, supper was served in the great hall of the castle, at which, for the entertainment of the guests, a decorated chariot and ship were drawn in, containing viands for the later courses of the banquet. [60] No ill-timed jest spoilt the pleasure of the party, as on the occasion of the festivities in celebration of James's baptism; but this time, owing to the religious change in Scotland, no French representatives were present at Stirling.

A few months before he departed from Scotland to take possession of the English crown, James looked down from Stirling Castle upon a strange and striking spectacle. On December 21st, 1602, a band of riders, consisting mainly of women, was observed advancing from the west. It was seen that the principal members of the party were bearing bloodstained garments and were displaying them to view with the object of attracting attention. The procession wound its way up the castle hill, and at the King's command was admitted within the gates. Alexander Colquhoun of Luss was the leader of the company, and from him the King learned that a party of MacGregors had raided the lands of Glenfinlas in the Lennox, had plundered the farms of the Colquhoun tenants, and had killed and wounded a number of men, and that these women bearing the bloody shirts were the relatives of the clansmen who had innocently suffered.

The sorrowing deputation and the accompanying tale of woe so greatly shocked King James that he granted a commission to Alexander Colquhoun, giving him licence to repress such crimes and to lay hold of any malefactors. The knowledge that their enemies possessed this commission so enraged the MacGregors that they rose in great force to oppose the Colquhouns, and inflicted upon them a heavy defeat at the memorable conflict of Glenfruin. [61] Their triumph, however, although sweet for the moment, brought long and bitter sorrow to the victors, as they came to be regarded as the most lawless of the Highland clans, and were pursued with fire and sword at the instance of the Government. To assist in crushing the indomitable race, the Earl of Mar, in 1611, sent two pieces of ordnance from Stirling Castle, to be used in the guerrilla warfare against the hunted Clan Gregor. [62]

James VI.'s son, Henry, was the last Prince of Scotland to be brought up in Stirling Castle. He spent nine years—exactly half of his life—in his royal birthplace on the rock. The King's former companion, the Earl of Mar, was appointed guardian of the boy, and Annabella, the Countess-Dowager, was authorised to assist her son in his charge. James had perfect confidence in the friend of his youth, but the Queen, partly, perhaps, from political motives and partly from a natural desire to be with her child, endeavoured in 1595 to remove the Prince from the custody of Mar. This intrigue becoming known to the sovereign led to a quarrel between him and his Consort, the result being that the Earl received a written statement from the King granting him full charge of the boy until he should reach the age of eighteen years:—"1595, July 24. Stirling.—Milorde of Mar. Because in the suretie of my sonne consistis my suretie and that I have concreditid unto you the chairge of his keiping upon the trust I have of youre honestie, this present thairfore sall be ane warrande unto you not to delyver him out of youre handis except I commande you with my awin mouth, and being in sikke cumpanie as I my self sall best lyke of, otheruayes not to delyver him for any chairge or message that can cum from me. And in kayce God call me at any tyme that nather for Quene nor Estaitis pleasure ye delyver him quhill he be auchtein yeiris of age and that he commande you himself. At Stirling the xxiiij of Julie, 1595. James R." [63]

The Queen succeeded in a later attempt to gain possession of her son. After James had set out for England to occupy Elizabeth's throne, she made her way to Stirling in April, 1603, in order to seize the person of the Prince. The family of Mar, refusing to deliver their charge, even when a band of nobles appeared in support of the Queen, Anne, in her disappointment, fell dangerously ill, whereupon the King dispatched the Duke of Lennox with instructions to the Earl of Mar to deliver the Prince to the Duke. [64] In order to appease the Queen, Lennox and the Council handed the boy to his mother, who at once began her journey with her son, reaching Windsor at the end of June, after a progress of more than four weeks.

On his father's accession to the English throne, the Prince of Scotland at once became Duke of Cornwall, and almost immediately after his arrival in England he was invested with the Order of the Garter. Not until 1610 was young Henry created Prince of Wales, a title which he was destined to enjoy for little more than two years. In October, 1612, he began to suffer from headaches and languor, but always making light of bodily ailments, he continued to lead an active life and to play his favourite games. Fever, however, most probably typhoid, compelled him to take to his bed. The best physicians were in attendance during his illness, but from the first there was little hope of recovery, and on the 6th of November he lost his speech and peacefully passed away.

So much beloved was the Prince by the people, and such a sensation did his early death create, that nearly all the eminent authors of the day, and many undistinguished mourners, wrote verses extolling his virtues and lamenting his demise. Donne, Heywood and Drummond of Hawthornden, were among the poets whose elegies were called forth by the national bereavement. Henry was a young man of great force of character, who held strong opinions on the topics of the day, and who did not fear to speak out his mind concerning some of his father's actions. He was naturally of a religious disposition, being strict in his attendance at the services of the Church, and his own deliberations on the different forms of faith led him to become a stronger Protestant than James. Kind-heartedness was one of Henry's characteristics. His pedagogue in the early Stirling days had been Adam Newton, a man whom the Prince always held in the highest esteem. Newton continued to discharge the duties of tutor after the Royal Family had migrated to England, but, like William Dunbar at the Court of James IV., he longed to be presented to an ecclesiastical benefice. In January, 1606, His Royal Highness sent a letter to the King, reminding him of his promise to give preferment to the tutor, and stating that for two years past Master Newton had been looking for the Deanery of Durham. James complied with his son's request, and in September the faithful tutor was rewarded with the coveted position. [65]

Steadfast attachment to his early friends was a feature of Henry's character. When an infant in Stirling Castle, he had been lovingly cared for by David Murray the attendant who slept in his chamber. The trusty Scot followed his young master to England and the friendship between them grew closer as the Prince advanced in years, till at last, when the fatal fever had rendered him almost speechless, he called out repeatedly for David. When Murray approached the bed the dying youth recognised his life-long companion, but sighed as he muttered again and again "I would say somewhat but I cannot utter it." [66]

According to the French ambassador, de la Boderie, Henry spent less time in study than in out-of-door exercise and games. "None of his pleasures," says the Ambassador, writing when the boy was little more than twelve, "savour the least of a child. He is a particular lover of horses and what belongs to them; but is not fond of hunting; and when he goes to it, it is rather for the pleasure of galloping, than that which the dogs give him. He plays willingly enough at Tennis, and at another Scots diversion [golf] very like mall; but this always with persons elder than himself, as if he despised those of his own age. He studies two hours a day, and employs the rest of his time in tossing the pike, or leaping, or shooting with the bow, or throwing the bar, or vaulting or some other exercise of that kind; and he is never idle. He shows himself likewise very good natured to his dependants, and supports their interests against any persons whatever; and pushes what he undertakes for them or others, with such zeal, as gives success to it." [67]

The Frenchman was probably wrong in supposing that the Prince played golf with persons older than himself because he despised those of his own age. The likelihood is that, as golf was introduced into England by Scotsmen who went south with James, only amongst his father's northern courtiers would Henry be able to find opponents and partners for his game. An anecdote of the Prince regarding golf is told by Strutt in *The Sports and Pastimes of the People of England*. "At another time playing at goff, a play not unlike to pale-maille, whilst his schoolmaster stood talking with another, and marked not his highness warning him to stand farther off, the prince thinking he had gone aside, lifted up his goff-club to strike the ball; mean tyme one standing by said to him, 'beware that you hit not master Newton': wherewith he drawing back his hand, said, 'Had I done so, I had but paid my debts.'" Henry's remark seems to infer that good Master Newton had not spared the rod in the course of his tutorial duties, just as George Buchanan, a generation earlier, did not shrink from chastising the Prince's father in the schoolroom at Stirling Castle.

The departure of Prince Henry for the south, after his father had come to his new inheritance, marks the end of the history of Stirling Castle as a regular dwelling-place of royalty. The ancient seat of monarchy was seldom occupied by princes after James had made his progress to London; but from time to time distinguished persons were lodged in the forsaken pile, albeit their stay within the fortress was not of their own seeking. In November, 1604, John, fifth Earl of Cassillis, was brought as a prisoner to Stirling from Blackness, his offence being that in the course of a dispute with his wife he attacked her in the presence of the Privy Council and dragged her out of the chamber. As the nobleman soon repented of his deed and sent a letter expressing his contrition to the Council, he was released from the castle at the end of the year, but was forbidden to pass further east than Linlithgow. [68]

In the following year Stirling Castle received as prisoners men of lowlier rank but of loftier spirit than Cassillis. These were several Presbyterian ministers, who, with others that were warded in Blackness, had attended the Assembly at Aberdeen in 1605, although the Privy Council, at James's instigation had forbidden all persons to appear at such a meeting. For about one year the disobedient clergymen were detained in the castle by the King. [69]

James at this time was inclined for little toleration towards either Presbyterians or Roman Catholics. In 1608, George, first Marquis of Huntly, was warded in Stirling Castle for refusing to abjure the Romish religion, and for alleged disloyalty, while for the same reasons the Popish Earl of Erroll was placed in confinement in Edinburgh. [70] After enduring imprisonment for many months, Huntly and Erroll wrote to their sovereign vainly beseeching him to grant them liberty, "for the King (as the treuth was) thought that he could not preserue the publicke peace better, then be keiping thesse birdes of prey so caidget wpe." [71] In the beginning of 1610, however, the Marquis was released on the understanding that henceforward he should embrace the Protestant faith.

Just about the time of Huntly's discharge the Earl of Mar, in his capacity of Sheriff of Stirlingshire, placed in the Palace at Stirling Castle a man named John Murray, who was charged with murder or manslaughter. The delinquent should have been lodged in the Tolbooth of the town, but the magistrates, "being movid with some foolishe

THE CHAPEL ROYAL.

consait," as Mar complained to the Privy Council, refused to concern themselves with the Sheriff's prisoners, and so he was obliged to turn the King's Palace into a common gaol. However, the Lords of Council listened to the Earl's petition and ordered the Stirling magistrates to receive in future such persons as he should apprehend. [72]

James was once again to reside in the home of his early days. Before leaving Scotland he had promised his people that he would return to his native land every three years; but only once in the course of his English reign did he pass within the borders of his northern kingdom. The summer of 1617 was the season chosen for the visit. Edinburgh, Dundee, St. Andrews and Glasgow were honoured by the presence of the King, and the inhabitants of Stirling had twice an opportunity of according welcome to their sovereign. The early days of July were spent by James in the familiar castle, and again towards the end of the month he came to reside in the Palace.

It was at the time of this, his last, visit to the castle that he heard the Regents of Edinburgh College discourse on the various branches of philosophy. A rumour had gone abroad that James intended to suppress the Universities of Aberdeen and Edinburgh, leaving the more ancient St. Andrews and Glasgow to be the Oxford and Cambridge of Scotland. [73] The Regents had desired to address the King at Edinburgh, but as no opportunity was given to them in the capital they made the journey to Stirling, hoping, doubtless, to impress him with their erudition and to justify the existence of their college. The scene of the disputation was the Chapel of the castle, where, on the evening of the 19th of July, a number of Scottish and English lords assembled with the King. Speeches were delivered in Latin and Greek, the pronunciations of the ancient tongues being after the Scottish mode, so that James took occasion to call the Englishmen's attention to the superior grace which the languages acquired when spoken in the manner prevalent north of the Tweed.

The King was highly pleased with the discussion, and after supper he summoned the Principal and Regents. The fears of the Professors as to the future of their seat of learning were dispelled at this evening interview, for James graciously offered himself as Patron of their institution, giving it the name of King James's College, and granting permission for the placing of his coat-of-arms on the gate of the humble building.

James's two brief sojourns at Stirling gave the inhabitants a taste of the glory that had formerly belonged to their town, while his residence in the castle after an absence of fourteen years must have brought again to his own mind a throng of gay and gloomy memories. The Park recalled the summer hours spent in his favourite pastime of hunting; the Keep reminded him of weary tasks and the rigid discipline of George Buchanan; the Chapel, where he listened to the Edinburgh Regents, had been the scene of his eldest child's baptism—that promising son who did not live to see again the place of his birth and early training. Young Mar's revolution and the second Raid of Stirling were events of too stirring a kind to be forgotten, and the King doubtless felt as he recalled his early reign that although his responsibilities had increased with his accession to the English throne, his life and liberty were less at his subjects' mercy than in the days when he reigned over Scotland alone.

STIRLING CASTLE.

From Engraving by Robert Sayer, 1753

Chapter Six - Later History

In the times when the King of Scots' capital was Edinburgh, a royal visit to Stirling was an occurrence of an ordinary kind. Preparations were made in the interior of the castle for the housing of the Court, but naturally the sovereign's arrival was not regarded as an event of historic importance. After the Union of the Crowns, however, when the royal family was domiciled in England, and the people in the north had grown unaccustomed to the sight of a monarch's pomp, a visit of the King to his ancient castle was eagerly looked forward to by the inhabitants of Stirling, and elaborate preparations were undertaken for his reception both within and without the building.

King Charles I. was a native of Scotland, but he left his fatherland when a child of tender years, and although he was anxious to travel north with James when that monarch obeyed what he called his salmon-like instinct, not until 1633 did Charles set foot again upon Scottish soil. Each year after his accession to the throne his northern subjects had expected his arrival, but time after time their sanguine hopes had been doomed to disappointment. In November, 1631, the Privy Council believed that Charles's promised visit was at length near at hand. Not only were the royal apartments at Stirling made ready for the King, but, in order that he might enjoy the sport his father loved, the hunting of hares was strictly forbidden within eight miles of the castle. At last, when Charles had finally made up his mind to venture into Scotland, the Privy Council reissued the decree regarding the protection of ground game. [74] The townspeople of Stirling, however, were to have but poor reward for their long and patient waiting. During his Scottish visit in 1633, the King passed two nights in the castle in the beginning of July, as he journeyed from Edinburgh to Fife and Perth, and when a few days later he returned to the Scottish capital he avoided the detour by the Old Bridge of Forth and crossed the Firth in a storm. [75]

The outbreak of the Great Civil War brought Stirling Castle again to the front. The Covenanting party being dominant at the time, Parliament decreed in 1640 that the fortresses should be placed in the charge of trusty natives of Scotland, although the Earl of Mar was not deprived of his heritable right to the custody of the castle. [76] In this year Archibald, Earl of Argyll, while endeavouring to force the Covenant on the Highlanders of Central Scotland, seized the Earl of Atholl in his camp in Strathtay and sent him prisoner to Stirling Castle. [77] After a brief stay in the fortress, however, the nobleman was conveyed to the capital, where an agreement was entered into by which he recovered his freedom.

In 1644 the great Marquis of Montrose began his brilliant series of military successes. Not only did the Highland clans rise, as always, for the House of Stewart, but a considerable body of Scoto-Irish troops had landed in the west to support the King's cause. After the Covenanters' defeat at Tippermuir the

Government began to be seriously alarmed, and Sir Archibald Primrose, Clerk to the Privy Council, was ordered to write to Livingstone of Westquarter, urging him to look well after the town, castle and bridge of Stirling, in case the Irish soldiers should take their route that way. [78] The castle, however, though garrisoned and prepared, did not figure in the wars of Montrose; for the Marquis turned northwards after Tippermuir, and when he eventually descended on the Lowlands he crossed the Forth by the Fords of Frew and not by Stirling Bridge.

Although the "Great Marquis" suffered death for his devotion to the King, the cause for which he laid down his life was not lost in his native country. In 1650 Charles II., a young man of twenty, landed at the mouth of the Spey, and although England at the time was under the Protectorate, the youthful adventurer was crowned King of Scots. In the end of July he spent some nights in Stirling Castle, delighting the townsfolk with his courtly manners and reminding the old inhabitants of the splendid days that had gone. Charles was the last of a long line of monarchs to take up residence within the old walls. A few months later Holburne, the captain of the castle, was suspected of being a Royalist only by pretence, and of having held treacherous communications with some of the agents of Oliver Cromwell. The officer obeyed the summons to appear before the Parliament of Perth, and there he succeeded in clearing himself of the charge which his enemies had brought up against him. [79]

Young King Charles did not long enjoy the ancient crown of his fathers. Cromwell's victories of Dunbar and Worcester made the continuance of the monarchy impossible, although all the Scottish strongholds did not at once surrender to the rule of the Protector. Under the governorship of Colonel William Conyngham—who as an undoubted Royalist had been placed in Holburne's position—the garrison of Stirling Castle determined to hold the fortress for the King. This defiance brought General Monk to the gates, with over five thousand men, on August 6th, 1651. The day after his arrival he ordered his soldiers to raise earthen platforms for mounting his guns. One of these batteries was erected in the churchyard, whence for three days a fire was kept up, causing considerable damage to the castle. At the same time Colonel Conyngham's ordnance played hard upon the graveyard platform: a cannonade that has left its traces on the church to the present day. On the fourteenth of the month, owing to a mutiny in the garrison, the governor sent out a letter to Monk desiring a treaty of surrender, although two days before, not foreseeing this contingency, he had told the besiegers that he would hold the fortress as long as he could. [80]

It was agreed that the castle should be handed over to Monk, that the prisoners in the building should be released, and that the garrison should be allowed to march out. Also that noblemen, gentlemen and inhabitants of the town, whose goods were in the castle, should have liberty to transport their property to other places. [81] Forty pieces of ordnance and twenty-six barrels of powder, along with a large number of barrels of beef and beer and many vessels of claret, fell into the hands of the besiegers. The spoils of the castle included also two coaches, the Earl of Mar's coronet and his robes of Parliament, and some of the King's hangings. The national records which had been preserved in the fortress were sent to the Tower of London. Some were returned to Scotland a few years later; others were lost at sea shortly after the Restoration.

Colonel Reade was left by General Monk in charge of Stirling Castle; and in his plan for the defence of Scotland, which he laid before the Protector in 1657, Monk proposed to garrison Stirling with thirteen companies of foot and a regiment of horse. [82] The Erskines' right to the custody of the fortress was overlooked by Oliver Cromwell, but after the Restoration, in 1661, Parliament granted to John, Earl of Mar and his heirs male, the governorship of the castle with its parks and pasturage and their rents and duties. [83] Quarter of a century later King James VII., angry at Earl Charles's opposition to his plans for the relief of Roman Catholics, deprived the nobleman of part of his hereditary right; but when William of Orange ascended the throne the keeping of the castle, with all the privileges attached to the office, was again entrusted to the family of Mar.

During the reign of Charles II. Stirling Castle was notable as a prison. All kinds of offenders—persons convicted of treason, holders of unlawful conventicles, disturbers of the public peace—were placed in ward in the fortress. One of these prisoners was Patrick Gillespie, who as a staunch supporter of Cromwell, had been made Principal of Glasgow University. On Charles's return he craved pardon through his wife for his anti-monarchical conduct, but in September, 1660, he was confined in Stirling Castle, [84] although in March of the following year he was released from a rigorous captivity.

Sir Patrick Hume of Polwarth was another of Charles II.'s distinguished prisoners. In 1673 he had spoken "with abundance of freedom and plainness" against the Duke of Lauderdale's policy; [85] and two years later he petitioned against and refused to pay for the support of, the garrison which was stationed in his shire in order to curb the Covenanters. Consequently, in 1675-6, he was compelled to spend some months in Stirling Castle, and a year or two later he was warded there again, though his wife was allowed to be with him.

Although Charles II. never saw Stirling after his Restoration, his brother James, the heir-presumptive, visited the castle in 1681. During the time of his sojourn in Scotland he resided chiefly at Holyroodhouse, but his interest in Linlithgow and Stirling was such that he determined to make a progress to those ancient seats in the early days of February. The weather, indeed, had been uncommonly mild, but on the 3rd of the month, when the Duke of Albany and York set forth from Holyrood, accompanied by John Churchill, afterwards the famous Duke of Marlborough, the ground was covered with a heavy coat of snow. James arrived at Stirling that evening, and passed the night, not, as would have been appropriate, in the palace of his fathers, but in Argyll's Lodging on the Castle Hill. Next day he was conducted round the royal fortress after the great guns had fired a salute and the Earl of Mar, with the garrison under arms, had received him at the gate. The Duke examined all the important rooms in the Palace and inspected the castle walls; he expressed his admiration for the buildings and for the situation of the fortress, as well as for the extensive prospect of the windings of the river and the country through which it meandered. He remarked that he had been told a great deal about that noble seat, but that it much exceeded all that he had heard of it. "It was," His Highness said, "inherent and natural to all the Royal Family for many years past to have a particular kindness for Strivling." As James departed from the castle the guns again sounded a salute. Next day he travelled back to Holyrood. [86]

Coming events do not always cast their shadows before. As the heir-presumptive to the British throne walked round the castle with Mar he did not foresee that soon, as King, he would curtail the privileges which the Earl enjoyed as governor of Stirling, and that the hereditary office would be fully restored by the supporters of the man who was to tear his crown from his brow. Nor could he picture to himself his grandson, a disinherited prince, striving to recover this bulwark of the north from the servants of an alien sovereign.

Rivers winding in rich valleys were favourite scenes with James. When an exile in France he used to enjoy the view of the Seine from the terrace of St. Germain, partly because of its intrinsic beauty and partly because it reminded him of the prospect of the Thames from Richmond Hill. Doubtless his thoughts often travelled to Scotland too, and the Seine must sometimes have brought to his mind the tortuous river that he once admired from the ramparts of Stirling Castle.

As the Restoration sent Patrick Gillespie into captivity at Stirling, so the Revolution brought the fourth Earl of Perth a prisoner into the castle. Earl James had been one of Scotland's leading men under the last Stewart king; but the days of his prosperity were brought to a close with the flight of his sovereign in 1688, and as he had espoused the Roman Catholic faith and had profited by the King's dispensing power, he had only punishment to expect at the hands of his political opponents. After an attempt to flee the country he was thrown into Stirling Castle, where he lay a prisoner till 1693. At first the Earl was somewhat harshly treated, but on his Countess's petitioning against his want of privacy the Estates agreed to relieve him of the constant attendance of his guards. [87]

Although Queen Anne never saw Stirling Castle, her name is associated with the fortifications that were constructed outside the gateway which James IV. had built. This addition consists of massive embrasured walls with outlook turrets, and an archway bearing the initials A. R. surmounted by a crown. The probability, however, is that the battery existed before the time of Anne, but that during her reign it was repaired and strengthened, an extra protection being the fosse. Thus the castle was fortified for the Jacobite rebellion that was yearly expected and dreaded, but that did not break out until 1715, a year after the death of the Queen.

On the accession of George I., John, Earl of Mar, being suspected of having Jacobite sympathies, was deprived of the governorship of Stirling Castle. Since that time the office of hereditary keeper has never been revived. The new King's prompt action not unnaturally strengthened the Jacobite predilections of the Earl, who awaited a favourable opportunity of raising the standard of James VIII.

In Mar's insurrection of 1715, as in former days, Stirling, with its bridge and castle, was a valuable military post. King George's Government lost little time in concentrating forces upon it, in order to prevent the Highland Jacobites from joining their friends in the south. In the end of August the royal army under General Wightman encamped in the Park and secured the castle and the bridge. The Duke of Argyll, to whom the supreme command of the forces was given, arrived at Stirling on the

TURRET ON QUEEN ANNE'S BATTERY.

17th September, and before long found himself at the head of nearly four thousand men.

The insurgents proposed to cross the Forth by detaching a portion of their army for the apparent purpose of effecting a passage at Stirling, and by sending their main body by the upper fords while the Royalists were engaged at the bridge. Argyll, however, having heard of his enemies' intentions, determined to take the initiative. Marching out of Stirling on November 12th, he blocked the Highlanders' way at Sheriffmuir, where on the following day an indecisive battle was fought. The right wing of each army was successful, and

52

both sides claimed the victory, but as Mar was prevented from crossing the Forth the advantage really lay with Argyll. During the absence of the army at Sheriffmuir the town and castle of Stirling were garrisoned by five hundred volunteers from Glasgow, who had camped for nearly two months in the Park with Wightman's regular troops.

The next appearance of Stirling Castle in history is during the Rebellion of the Forty-five, although not until after the retreat from Derby did the enemy come before its gates. True, in September, 1745, the Highlanders passed so close to the castle that guns were fired from the battlements, but Charles was pushing on rapidly to Edinburgh and had no mind for a siege by the way. It was on the 6th of January, 1746, that the Highland army appeared again in the neighbourhood of Stirling. Charles Edward took up residence in Bannockburn House, while his soldiers camped in the vicinity, and on the same day the town of Stirling was summoned to surrender. Seeing no prospect of holding out against the dreaded mountaineers, the citizens capitulated on the 8th of the month, but the castle garrison under General Blakeney prepared to resist to the last extremity. To Charles's demand for the delivery of the fortress the General proudly replied that His Royal Highness must have a bad opinion of him to think him capable of surrendering the castle in such a cowardly manner. [88]

An engineer of the name of Grant had arranged to erect batteries in the old churchyard, as it occupied a high piece of ground, commanding the entrance to the castle. The citizens, however, objected to this plan, as General Blakeney's guns would have reduced their town to ruins. Charles therefore ordered the Frenchman, Mirabelle de Gordon, whom the soldiers ironically called Mr. Admirable, to undertake the siege operations. Mirabelle, according to the Chevalier Johnstone, had little knowledge of engineering and was totally destitute of judgment, discernment and commonsense; but because he was a French engineer, decorated with an order, it was supposed he was a person of experience, talents and capacity. The Frenchman began to dig trenches on the Gowan Hills, at a place where the solid rock was only fifteen inches below the surface of the ground, so that bags filled with wool and earth had to be brought from a distance to afford some sort of cover. The battery after all did little damage to the castle, and when Blakeney's guns were turned upon it Mirabelle's men were slaughtered in great numbers, and the position had soon to be abandoned. [89]

This ill-conducted siege was an unsuccessful enterprise, but it gave to Charles's Highlanders their victory at Falkirk. History never repeats itself, but sometimes it nearly does so. As Edward II. had marched to Bannockburn in order to relieve the Castle of Stirling, so General Hawley advanced by the same route from Edinburgh for the purpose of saving the same ancient stronghold from falling into the hands of Bruce's descendant. Charles left the Duke of Perth with over a thousand men to continue the blockade while the rest of the army barred the way near Bannockburn, as King Robert had done long before; but finding that Hawley was in no haste to attack,

Charles quitted the field of happy omen and advanced to unpropitious Falkirk. The memory of Wallace's defeat, however, did not oppress the eager Highlanders, for they routed the Government troops in a storm of wind and rain, and drove them back on Linlithgow. After this victory Charles returned to Stirling to proceed with the siege of the castle, and twice on the day of his arrival the garrison was summoned to surrender. Blakeney, however, answered that he had always been looked upon as a man of honour, and that the rebels should find that he would die so. [90] In their desperation a number of Highlanders tried to scale the castle rock, but they were driven back with heavy loss of life in their daring attempt to imitate the feats of medieval warriors. The chiefs at length saw the hopelessness of the undertaking, and with difficulty managed to persuade their Prince—who at times was bravely exposing himself to the fire of the garrison's guns—to withdraw his troops to the Highland hills. On February 1st the army began its disorderly retreat, taking the road to the Fords of Frew, for Blakeney had some time before destroyed the south arch of the old Bridge of Forth, and next day the Duke of Cumberland, who had superseded Hawley, entered and occupied Stirling town.

To many people the history of Scotland seems to cease with the suppression of the Rebellion of Forty-five. This idea doubtless takes its rise from the fact that no battle has been fought on Scottish soil since the Jacobites were vanquished by Cumberland. Up to that point strife and bloodshed are so characteristic of the nation's history, that the important half-centuries that have elapsed since Culloden are apt to be considered as having no connection with the story that began in the early ages and ended when "Prince Charlie" took ship at Lochnanuagh. Yet because royalty has forsaken its former seat, and because in times of peace a fortress cannot play a glorious part, the retiral of the Highlanders in 1746 does mark the close of Stirling Castle's long and noble history.

Since that time the building has been used as barracks and has become a recruiting depot for the Argyll and Sutherland Highlanders. Once or twice in the course of the nineteenth century its former days were recalled. In 1820, Hardie and Baird, two prominent leaders in the "Radical War," were imprisoned in the castle before their execution, like Archbishop Hamilton and other political offenders in the times of the Stewart kings. On the 13th of September, 1842, the pleasanter days of the past were brought to mind when the presence of Queen Victoria and Prince Albert within the walls revived the old associations of royalty. Seventeen years later their son, the Prince of Wales, inspected the ancient building where his ancestors had lodged, and from the spot where his mother had surveyed the scene, he admired the view which kings have enjoyed of the Vale of Menteith and the Highland hills. To Queen Victoria and her son thoughts must have occurred similar to those which passed through the mind of James, Duke of Albany and York, when he observed that it was inherent and natural to all the Royal Family to have a particular kindness for Stirling.

Chapter Seven - The Buildings, The Park and The Bridge

The castle that stands on Stirling rock to-day is not the building that was the home of Alexander I. and William the Lion. Their royal dwelling was thrown into ruins in the days of the devastating War of Independence. Robert the Bruce's invariable policy was to destroy all fortresses that fell into his hands, lest they should be captured again by the English and made the seats of oppression; so that most of the castellated buildings that had escaped destruction before Bannockburn were cast down or dismantled soon after that battle. In 1336, when the Southrons were again overrunning distracted Scotland, King Edward III. ordered the castle to be repaired and fortified, and it is possible that some of the work then done has lasted to the present day. A portion of the north-west structure, overlooking the steepest part of the rock, may date from the time when Thomas de Rokeby held Stirling for Edward III.

Throughout the reigns of the Stewart monarchs money was spent on mason-

PORTCULLIS IN JAMES IV.'S GATEWAY.

work at the castle, but it is impossible to say with certainty for how much of the building each king was responsible. It seems clear, however, that the ancient gateway, afterwards built up, leading to Ballengeich, was erected by Robert II., for the *Exchequer Rolls* of 1380–1 mention the construction at Stirling Castle of a barbican and a northern gate. This was apparently the main entrance to the fortress; but either because the approach to the inner ward

55

was found to be too steep, or because a later building—perhaps the Parliament Hall—partly obstructed the way, a new gateway was made beside the older one, and a twisted tunnel was boldly cut through the lower storey of the Mint—a building which was probably the "cunyie-house" of the early Stewarts, and which seems to have been erected at the same time as the original archway. There is little doubt also that important additions were made during James III.'s reign. Certainly the castle wall was rebuilt in 1467, [91] and the likelihood is that it remains to the present day in the part above the Prince's Walk and in the portion of similar construction overlooking Ballengeich.

The splendid building called the Parliament Hall indicates by its style of architecture that it belongs to a period corresponding to the reign of James III., and tradition is doubtless correct in ascribing its design to the ill-fated Cochrane who was hanged by the nobles at Lauder Bridge. This great hall unfortunately suffered at the hands of the military authorities when they converted it into barracks towards the end of the eighteenth century,

THE OLD MINT.

but even with all its defacements it is still a building of noble proportions. Taylor, the Water-Poet, who saw it in 1618, wrote that "it surpasses all the halls for dwelling-houses that ever I saw, for length, breadth, height and strength of building." On the east and west sides the windows have been ruthlessly modernised, but those in the south end remain unaltered, showing their simple moulding and remarkable deep recesses. The oriel facing east, towards the south end of the hall, preserves much of its former beauty, its

56

most interesting features being the interlacing of the moulded jambs of the now built-up side lights. The tower on the east side containing the stair is still a prominent feature of the building, although it is not now crowned by its steep-pitched conical roof. A covered passage formerly extended along the west side of the edifice, but—like the majority of the figures that filled the niches on the walls—it has not survived the harsh treatment to which the Parliament Hall was subjected. The corners of this great pile were formerly adorned with turrets, but these with the rest of the building were allowed to go to decay, and were removed when the hall was repaired for use as barracks. The stones of the south gable bear numerous scars like bullet-marks, which possibly date from the siege of 1746. The Highlanders on that occasion climbed to the roofs of the houses in the town, and thence discharged their small arms at the fortress that so resolutely kept at bay the enemies of King George.

The portcullis gateway leading to the lower courtyard from the outer works was erected by James IV. [92] This fore-entry is not now so imposing as it was in the days of the Stewart sovereigns, for instead of the two stumps of towers now remaining there were formerly four high bastion-like structures. This part of the castle received some damage from the guns of General Monk, but although the towers suffered at the time of the siege, they were standing many years afterwards. Gradually, however, they crumbled into ruins until repairs were undertaken to prevent further decay at about the beginning of the nineteenth century. The lowest chamber in each of these great towers was a dark and noisome dungeon. The vaulted passage of the gateway was provided at both the outer and the inner ends with portcullises, one of which still hangs in the small archway at the side of the principal entrance.

It has been thought that the Palace, the most important part of Stirling Castle, owes its origin to James IV. True, it is always spoken of as James V.'s building, but several extracts from the *Treasurer's Accounts* have led many to believe that the work was begun by the knight-errant monarch who fell on Flodden Field. Certainly, in 1496, Walter and John Merlioun, masons, were employed on the King's house in Stirling, and in the following year the master-mason of Linlithgow rode over to give his advice. If the Palace, however, had been merely begun by James IV. the *Treasurer's Accounts* would not have contained references to glass for the windows and to other furnishings for a nearly furnished building; [93] and it is obvious by the style of the architecture, which is the earliest Renaissance work in Scotland, that the work could not have been completed before the fifth James succeeded to the throne. The house that was being erected by John and Walter Merlioun may have been the tower called the Keep, an older and plainer edifice than the Palace to which it has been joined.

This building, then, was raised in the time of James V., the monarch during whose troubled reign the Renaissance style was introduced. The King's visit to France for his marriage with Princess Madeleine in 1537, may have increased his interest in the architecture of the day, but the royal dwelling at Stirling was probably designed before the date of that alliance, as Sir James Hamilton of Finnart, who was James's principal architect, and who is known to have worked at Stirling Castle, [94] had seen the French Renaissance structures twenty years before.

The Palace is an ornate edifice, showing a blending of the Gothic and the Classical designs. It is roughly in the form of a square, having a courtyard in the middle called the Lions' Den, where tradition says the royal animals were caged. The third and fourth Jameses certainly owned lions, and it is likely that their successor kept a specimen of the King of Beasts as much for his amusement as for an emblem of royal power. On the exterior of the Palace, between the windows—each of which is surmounted by a stone showing I 5 for James V.—are shallow niches containing ornamental pillars supporting statues which are now much defaced. The figure at the north-east corner of the building is thought to represent the King disguised as the "Gudeman o' Ballengeich," as above the head a lion holds the crown and a tablet inscribed I 5. Running round three sides of the Palace is an elaborately-carved cornice, upon which rests a series of short pillars, each one intended to bear a small statue, although some on the north are wanting. Towards the west the building presents an unfinished appearance; obviously it was meant to

JAMES V. AS "THE GUDEMAN O' BALLENGICH."

have additions on that side. The interior of the Palace has been greatly changed since the days of James V., but one or two noble fire-places still exist in the rooms that are now given over to the soldiers. More than one ancient door studded with iron has survived the alterations; but the beautiful carved

58

oak panels, representing members of the Royal Family and persons about the Court, and known as the Stirling Heads, were removed towards the end of the eighteenth century because one of them fell from its place in the ceiling and seriously injured a soldier. Tradition asserts, doubtless with truth, that the gratings were placed in the windows for the protection of young James VI., in the stormy days when raids on Stirling were events against which it was well to be guarded.

On the north side of the inner square stands the Chapel rebuilt by James VI. in 1594. This was the Chapel Royal of Scotland before King James carried out Queen Mary's wish and transferred the endowments and the epithet "Royal" to the chapel of Holyroodhouse. It is a somewhat plain Renaissance structure, having externally much the same appearance as when it was newly finished for Prince Henry's baptism. The Chapel, however, has been put to so many secular uses that the interior now bears no resemblance to a place of worship, and it is hard to believe that within these walls a brilliant congregation of nobles assembled to witness the christening of an heir to two crowns.

The *Exchequer Rolls* and other sources of information contain many entries referring to the payment of chaplains in Stirling Castle, and some of those records imply that for a considerable period two ecclesiastical buildings were maintained on the top of the rock. The Collegiate Church of Stirling was not the same edifice as that which was known as the Old Kirk in the castle. The truth seems to be that when James III. determined to erect a Chapel Royal and Collegiate Church he chose a new site for this building, and not the one occupied by the Kirk of St. Michael, where he and his fathers had worshipped. There were two chapels in Stirling Castle as late as the second half of the sixteenth century, [95] but to-day no walls remain above the ground to point out the position of old St. Michael's Church. Its site was probably the high part of the rock near the north-west angle of the Palace. The building that James VI. re-erected in 1594 doubtless rests on the foundations of James III.'s Collegiate Church.

The part of the castle containing the Douglas Room was largely destroyed by fire in the middle of the nineteenth century, and has been restored in a style out of keeping with its surroundings, but the closet with the window through which the Earl's body was flung did not share the fate of the neighbouring apartments on the night of the conflagration.

The present outer gateway of Stirling Castle is a comparatively modern structure. It was probably erected in the first half of the eighteenth century in view of the expected Jacobite rebellion. The inner barrier with the initials of Queen Anne is naturally supposed to date from that monarch's reign, but the probability is that the fortifications were only strengthened in the early eighteenth century, for Slezer's views of the castle in 1693 show walls and turrets similar to those now known as Queen Anne's, and as Slezer records that the battery was at that time in course of erection, it is unlikely that it would have needed rebuilding only some ten years later. This bulwark of William and Mary's reign probably succeeded an earlier fortification in near

THE PROSPECT OF THEIR MAJESTIES' CASTLE OF STIRLING.

From Engraving by Captain John Slezer, 1693.

ly the same situation, for the French or Spur Battery would not likely have been erected beyond the outer gate of the castle, and the Prince's Walk, with the adjacent lawn, was almost certainly protected by a wall before the last decade of the seventeenth century.

The Nether Bailey was never much built upon, and does not now contain any interesting structures. The name, meaning the "lower fortified enclosure," is derived through the late Latin *ballium*, from *vallum*, a fortification or rampart.

As a water supply within the walls was essential to every medieval castle, the well in many fortresses is the oldest piece of work that has come down to the present day. Stirling Castle possesses two wells, both of them of great antiquity, but the probability is that the one in the Outer Square is older than that in the Nether Bailey. The earliest stronghold doubtless occupied only the higher part of the rock, and when in later times the lower ledge was enclosed the additional well would be made. Both founts are known to have been used before the middle of the fourteenth century, but the older one must have been hewn out of the rock many hundreds of years earlier than the days of David Bruce. To-day the wells in Stirling Castle are not exposed to view, but it is likely that in the near future one at least will be uncovered, and will remain open as of yore.

The first mention of a royal park connected with Stirling Castle occurs in the reign of King William the Lion. That monarch, as has already been stated, acknowledged in a charter to the monks of Dunfermline that he had appropriated some of their land when he first enclosed the chase. This piece of ground, to the south-west of the castle, was afterwards known as the Old Park to distinguish it from another royal hunting-field made by Alexander III. The New Park of King Alexander lay to the south of the other, and its position brought it prominently into history at the time of the Battle of Bannockburn.

Towards the end of his life King Robert the Bruce granted the lands of Old Park and New Park to his faithful servant, Adam the Barber; [96] but during David Bruce's reign the estates by some means became for a time Sir Robert Erskine's property. The King resumed possession of the royal domains by giving Erskine in exchange the lands of Alloa and others, but soon afterwards David bestowed the New Park on Alexander Porter, who was obliged to present to the King every year *arcum cum uno circulo pro alaudis*—a bow and apparently a snare for catching larks. A portion of the Old Park was granted by James IV. to the burgesses of Stirling in compensation for the lands of Gallowhills (or Gowan Hills), which they had allowed him to enclose. [97] The table-land lying to the south-west of the castle rock is known to this day as the King's Park, and, along with the Gowan Hills, is still the property of the Crown.

As a short cut to the Park and to the King's Stables, which lay not far from the village of Raploch, a path was made in 1531 down the steep hillside from the north-west angle of the castle. The built-up doorway can still be seen in the wall of the Nether Bailey, and it was doubtless by this postern that the boy James VI. passed out to hunt on the summer day of 1579 when his wardens allowed him to go forth without a guard.

It is not until the latter half of the fifteenth century that the Royal Gardens at Stirling become important enough to demand attention. In earlier days there was probably a piece of ground set apart for horticultural purposes on the top of the castle rock, but not before the reign of James III. do gardens on an extensive scale appear to have been laid out. In the *Exchequer Rolls* of that King's time there are numerous entries of payments to James Wilson, the keeper of the garden at Stirling Castle; indeed, the unfortunate *dilettante* monarch was almost as much interested in his plants and fruit-trees as in architecture, music and astrology. This King and his successor, James of the Iron Belt, wrought great improvements in the pleasure grounds at Stirling. The father made a new royal garden, which probably lay on the sloping land close to the old Round Table; and the son extended the horticultural area by including a portion of the adjoining meadow and thus embracing the ancient mound. James IV. was more versatile than his father, and he showed his warlike nobles that devotion to gardening and other peaceful occupations was not incompatible with interest in military affairs. The new enclosure was stocked with plum-trees, pear-trees, vines and vegetables, as well as strawberries and flowers. There was in the Park a small natural loch to the south of the Round Table, but James IV. seems to have made ponds or canals beside his new beds and terraces, for the garden was not only an orchard, it was also a pleasant retreat for the King and the lords and ladies of the Court. The clergy of the Chapel Royal took over the charge of the horticulture, and sent men to different parts of Scotland to procure the best seeds and plants.

The Round Table which formed the middle point of James IV.'s new garden was probably in ancient days a place for holding tribal assemblies. In early feudal times it seems to have been the centre of the King's Ward, which was the muster-ground where armed vassals presented themselves to their sovereign. The *Exchequer Rolls* of James IV. state that the King changed the ward into a garden, and it was doubtless after this alteration that the place came to be spoken of as the Knot, although the old name continued to be used, for Sir David Lyndsay in James V.'s reign wrote of the "Tabyll Rounde." The Town Council of Stirling, thinking that the mound and terraces were in danger of becoming obliterated, repaired and slightly altered the King's Knot in the latter half of the nineteenth century.

The site of the tournament ground at Stirling has been a matter of dispute, some holding that the jousting took place on the flat land near the King's Knot, others maintaining that the hollow called the Valley, between the castle and the Ladies' Rock, was the scene of these chivalric encounters. The truth seems to be that although the Valley was used for games in the time of James VI., [98] the level ground below the hill was the place where the lists were set in the period of the early Stewart kings. This opinion is supported by the fact that the ground now covered by houses to the south-east of the King's Knot was formerly known by the significant name of the Justing (or Justin) Flats. It must have been on this level tract that the Douglases fought with the knights of Burgundy in the presence of James II., for in the Valley there would have been too little space for the lists, the champions' tents, the King's pavilion and the four thousand retainers brought by the Douglases to witness the encounter. The rock where tradition says the ladies sat to view the games and combats is much nearer to the Valley than to the Justin Flats, but it is probable that the high-born dames of the Court sat in the royal pavilion beside the lists, and that the rock was occupied by gentlewomen to whom the privilege was not granted of sitting beside the King. It may be, however, that the Ladies' Rock did not receive its name till Queen Mary's time or even till 1594, when the Valley was the scene of the sports which were held in celebration of Prince Henry's baptism.

The surroundings of the castle, like the buildings themselves, have undergone considerable changes since royalty resided in Stirling. No beds of flowers and fish ponds are now to be seen in the gardens of the Jameses: that piece of ground is somewhat like what it was before the Round Table became the King's Knot. Villas now stand on the once famous Justin Flats; the small Park Loch has been drained away; and the Ladies' Rock has suffered partial demolition to make room for the new cemetery that occupies the Valley. Ballengeich, or the "Windy Pass," on the other side of the castle, was deepened at the north-west end to afford a more gradual ascent for the road; and the Back Walk, leading from Ballengeich round the rock, although it had been begun a number of years before "Prince Charlie's" siege, was not completed till the eighteenth century had almost come to a close.

* * * * *

The old Bridge of Stirling, although half a mile distant from the summit of the rock, has been too closely associated with the history of the castle to be overlooked in even a brief description of the buildings and their surroundings. The fortress watched and guarded the bridge for three centuries and a half, as it had watched and guarded the earlier bridge which crossed the Forth about one hundred yards above the site of the later structure. The early edifice, which seems to have been a platform of wood on piers of stone, was the scene of Wallace's victory in 1297. During that great battle the beams gave way, plunging many soldiers into the river; and although Edward I. in 1305 issued a writ for the repair of the bridge, [99] it was apparently never rebuilt, as throughout the fourteenth century a ferry was in use at Stirling.

The stone bridge of four arches, which is still to be seen, was erected in the early days of the fifteenth century, but in the course of many ages it has undergone repairs and alterations. Under Robert III. the building was begun, and was finished by his brother, the Regent Albany, about the year 1415. Its appearance to-day is slightly less imposing than it was before the middle of the eighteenth century, for in former times the road passed through an archway at each end of the bridge—the northern one containing an iron gate—and the buttresses of the central pier rose above the parapet and were made to form small guardhouses for those who kept the gate. On the southern bank of the Forth, at the end of the bridge, stood the Chapel of St. Marrock or St. Roch, in which in pre-Reformation days kings and others made their offerings before passing over the stream. As the road approaches the river from the north, it is made to take a double twist, the object of this arrangement doubtless being to throw into confusion any body of cavalry intending to force a passage at this important spot. Probably for the same defensive purpose the bridge is not straight but is somewhat bow-shaped; it seems to sag as if it had felt the current's strain, for the centre is about a couple of feet further down the stream than the ends.

STIRLING OLD BRIDGE.

It may truly be said that Stirling Auld Brig has borne more men and women famous in Scotland's history than any other bridge in the kingdom. Every Scottish monarch, from James I. to Charles II., nine sovereigns in all, has crossed the Forth by those arches. To most of the kings and queens, as to the majority of the Scottish nobility, the bridge was as familiar as the castle. Because of its being a clasp connecting the north with the south, this structure was almost as valuable a military post as the stronghold which overlooks it. When the rebels closed the gates of the castle against King James III., they at the same time placed a force at the bridge in order to cut off communications between the sovereign and his northern friends. The royal forces, however, with more spirit than they showed a few days later at Sauchieburn, drove this company across the Bridge of Forth and pursued them as far as the house of Keir.

64

In later times, the Privy Council in Edinburgh, realising the importance of the bridge, ordered that it as well as the castle should be in a state of defence, for Montrose had won the battle of Tippermuir and his Scoto-Irish soldiers were expected to pass by way of Stirling. The Marquis, however, on his way to the south, avoided crossing the Forth near the castle, but his enemy, Baillie,

the Covenanting general, led his troops over the river by this bridge before his defeat by Montrose at Kilsyth. Again, on the outbreak of the Fifteen Rebellion, Wightman, the Hanoverian general, took possession of both bridge and castle, placing sentries in the former's guardhouses, as the object of the Government was to prevent the Highland Jacobites from joining their friends in the south. The bridge was prominent in military history for the last time during "Prince Charlie's" war. Its proximity to the garrisoned castle caused the Highlanders to cross the Forth at Frew, some eight miles up the river, and before they returned from England to the neighbourhood of Stirling, Blakeney had cut the south arch, so that when Cumberland pressed on their rear they could not retreat by the bridge. By throwing beams across the breach the Hanoverian soldiers were able to take the nearest way to the north, but three years elapsed before the broken arch was restored to its former condition.

The Forth is now spanned by many bridges, including a comparatively new one at Stirling, but from the days of the Regent Albany until the middle of the eighteenth century all traffic between north and south that went not by ford and ferry was supported by the four medieval arches. The Old Bridge of Stirling, although closed to vehicles, still bears passengers on foot; but its great days all belong to the past, though "Time, which antiquates antiquities," and has long ago given to it a venerable appearance, will not destroy the fabric for many years to come and will cherish its story for ever.

Chapter Eight - The Associations of the Buildings

In the preceding pages a description was given of the buildings of the castle as they stand at the present day. In this chapter the purpose is to remind the reader of the celebrated events that took place within or beside these existing edifices, and to enable him to picture to himself some of the scenes that have been enacted on the "well-trod stage" of Stirling rock.

Since the gay days of the Jameses, and still more since the troubled years of Robert Bruce, important changes have been wrought in the buildings that have occupied Snowdon Crag. War has done its work of destruction; government officials have disfigured noble halls; fire has eaten up the dwelling-rooms of kings; and monarchs themselves have sometimes thought it right to remove the ancient landmarks which their fathers had set. Yet there still remains at Stirling a large cluster of historical buildings sufficient to make the castle the most notable place of its kind in Scotland, if not in the British Isles.

The first thing to strike the visitor after he has passed through Queen Anne's gateway is the ancient Keep, with its corbelled turrets, that rises from the lawn and the Prince's Walk. Associations lend interest to the beauty, for

OLD ENTRANCE FROM BALLENGEICH.

there is the staircase leading to the schoolroom where George Buchanan taught and punished his wilful pupil, James VI., and on the terrace below the old wall that King's eldest son, Prince Henry, was accustomed to walk when released by his tutor for a few minutes' breathing-space in the fresh air. Other incidents are quickly brought to mind on this same approach to the castle.

66

Just in front is James IV.'s entrance, shorn, it is true, of its lofty towers, but still the same archway that witnessed, besides other memorable events, two striking scenes in the time of James V. The first was when Margaret Tudor, standing hand-in-hand with her son, the young King, rang down the portcullis in these self-same grooves, suddenly placing the ponderous grating between her precious child and the Regent Albany's dumfoundered commissioners. The second occurrence took place some years later when James had become a grown man. A panting horse clattered up the ascent, bearing a stern-eyed, hard-visaged monarch. At the side ran Archibald Douglas of Kilspindie, almost collapsing with fatigue, but gazing into the rider's face in his eagerness to catch a look of recognition. Here, at the entrance, Kilspindie sank down exhausted, while the King, unheeding, rode on through the archway into the castle yard. In his exile Douglas had thought the English people too proud, "and that they had too high a conceit of themselves, joined with a contempt and despising of all others." But his treatment at the hands of his sovereign and former friend must have been the bitterest experience of his life. No affront that he received in England had been harder to bear than this. It would be difficult to find in history a more cruel, silent rebuff.

On emerging from the tunnel gateway the stranger is confronted by the great imposing gable of the Parliament House. This building, although altered and much defaced, is still a majestic pile, and is noteworthy as having almost certainly been erected under the directorship of Cochrane, the architect, one of James III.'s unpopular favourites. Poor Cochrane was hanged at Lauder Bridge on the famous occasion when the Earl of Angus thought fit to "Bell the Cat," and show the King that Scottish nobles would not suffer art-loving upstarts to usurp the high places at Court. The quaint, twisted entrance below the old Mint, to the north of the Parliament House, was the way of approach to the castle up till the following reign, so that often in his later years, when James III. rode into his courtyard, he must have shuddered as he caught sight of the building that reminded him of Cochrane and his miserable fate.

The Palace, which is chief among Stirling Castle's buildings, can be viewed on one of its three elaborate sides from this same spot near James IV.'s gateway. Often must King James V. have walked about this ground while the walls of his stately house were rising, and many a day he doubtless stood watching the workmen shaping the pillars and carving the curious figures. Out of these windows, before they were barred, have looked Mary of Guise and the Regent Arran, and unhappy Queen Mary has lain within these walls weeping sorely at the hardness of her lot. Then came the time when the infant Prince James was brought for his safety to Stirling, the stronghold that was to become his home throughout his boyhood's years. Yet, in the turmoil of politics and religion, the royal child's anxious guardians felt that the strong position of the castle was not sufficient protection for their precious charge. Consequently, the windows on the main floor of the Palace were grated with heavy iron bars—the work, it is said, of a St. Ninian's blacksmith—which yet remain firmly fixed in their stones to remind the peace-loving generations of the perilous days of the past. Many a night has James VI. lain sleepless behind these gratings, dreading lest by the morning light he should be carried a prisoner to Edinburgh or Dumbarton.

From the upper square of the castle another side of the Palace can be examined, and from here can best be seen the corner statue of James V., disguised as "The Gudeman o' Ballengeich." The Parliament House, having been so much changed for the worse, is hardly worth regarding from this point of view; but the past can be recalled on the north side of the quadrangle, where stands the Chapel of James VI. Immediately after the re-erection of the building, that pillared doorway was thronged with a gay procession, pressing in to witness the baptism of baby Henry, the first-born son of the King of Scots. Great nobles of the kingdom as well as powerful lairds accompanied James and the foreign ambassadors into the sacred edifice; but the interior to-day has such a profaned appearance that even the most imaginative persons find it nearly impossible to picture to themselves the interesting religious ceremony. A number of years later, when James VI. returned from England to visit his native land, the Chapel was the scene of a long series of discourses, which the Regents or Professors of the Edinburgh College delivered to their sovereign in Latin and Greek. As the exterior of the building is almost precisely the same as it was when King James looked with pride upon it, so it is in the doorway again that the pedantic monarch can be summoned up as he slowly leaves the Chapel—where he had followed all the arguments—at the head of a company of courtiers and scholars.

Now let the visitor proceed to the Douglas Garden, a name that conjures up a passionate monarch's crime. The tall buildings overlooking the lawn do not contain the actual chamber where the Earl of Douglas supped with James II. Fire made away with most of the apartments in this interesting portion of the castle, but fortunately the little closet was spared where the King and his attendants stabbed the nobleman to death. There, above the old archway, it lies open to public view, and the window still exists through which the body was hurled after it had stained with blood the floor of the royal chamber. There is a grim fascination about that little room. The Earl of Douglas, the most powerful lord in Scotland, sat there and quietly but firmly refused to obey his sovereign's command, till James of the Fiery Face grew hot with indignation and suddenly put an end to the career of his over-powerful subject. The scene as the corpse was flung through the window, while the King stood by half angry and half afraid, can vividly be brought to mind even although the small apartment is not in appearance exactly as it was in the middle of the fifteenth century.

The walk round the wall of the Douglas Garden is in itself a sufficient attraction to bring passing travellers to the summit of the rock. The view is not one that is to be compared with others in Scotland only; it must have a place in the limited list of the world's most famous prospects. The great blue screen of the Highland mountains, including Ben Lomond, Ben Venue, Ben Ledi and Ben Vorlich, stretches from west to north with an outline of beautiful irregularity. Not in one long chain are the hills, but peak behind peak and row behind row, they appear as a compact phalanx of bens when the mist is lifted from off their heads. Nearer are the Braes of Doune and the fertile fields of the Vale of Menteith, in the midst of which the Forth can be seen gleaming in its lazy windings. The lofty Ochils in the north-east bring the Highlands near to Stirling and form a noble background to the historic Abbey Craig; and in the opposite direction the eye finds rest on the bleak Gargun-nock Hills, that serve to shut from the observer's mind the remembrance that a great city's turmoil lies not far beyond.

It is not, however, only for the beauty of the distant scene that the wall of the Douglas Garden must be sought; close beside the castle rock many spots of intense historical interest claim a share of attention. The battlefield of Stir-ling Bridge, where Wallace won his greatest victory, may be observed be-yond the Heading Hill—that dismal mound with its stone still showing the marks of the executioner's axe. Southwards from the scene of conflict the ancient tower of Cambuskenneth Abbey rises from between two reaches of the River Forth. Nearer, on the Gowan Hill, Edward I. placed the military en-gines that succeeded in breaching the castle wall; and on the same eminence, in 1746, the Jacobites planted a battery. Slightly further to the right is the hollow, now occupied by the houses of the Lower Castle Hill, where Friar Keillor set forth his play before King James V. On the other side of the rock the visitor will notice the extensive elevated tract of land known as the King's Park. There the Stewart monarchs and their predecessors found delight in the excitement of the chase; there the boy James II. was hunting when Crich-ton's men surrounded him and carried him to Edinburgh; there the youthful James VI., rejoicing in the freedom from his guardians and tutors, found such zest in his sport one summer day that he tarried till seven o'clock in the evening, having left the castle at the early hour of five. The field immediately below the rock on this south-west side of the castle was formerly known as the Butt Park, for in olden times it was the place appointed for the practice of archery and for shooting competitions. A little further south the eye can de-tect the ancient mound called the King's Knot, past which Edward II. rode when refused admittance to the castle after Bannockburn, and which in the days of the later Jameses formed the centre of an ornamental garden. On ac-count of the change that has come over it, the ground that was once the Jus-tin Flats makes little appeal to the imagination. Villas and gardens cover the level space where Douglases and Burgundian warriors fought for personal glory and national reputation in the presence of young James II.; but the flat nature of the land, well-suited for tournaments, can be made out beyond the King's Knot. The Field of Bannockburn, or that part of it where the first of the fighting took place, can be distinguished from the commanding position of the Douglas wall, and close beside the scene of Bruce's triumph may be dis-cerned the site of the battle of Sauchie, which resulted in King Robert's de-scendant, James III., fleeing to his death from the presence of his son.

The view from the castle could not fail to have some effect upon the minds of the monarchs who have gazed from the walls. To William the Lion, old and sick, the remembrance of the winding Forth and the purple peaks of Ben Lomond and Ben Ledi came as a light in the darkness, and he urged his attendants to carry him to Stirling that the breezes from the hills of the Lennox and Menteith might blow again upon his aged cheek. When James IV. looked out upon Ben Vorlich he was reminded of the merry hours of hunting near its base, and often did he plan an expedition to Glen Artney when the mountains in one of their genial moods tempted his eager spirit. The effect which the view had on James V. was to arouse in that "King of the Commons" the desire to become acquainted with the customs of the people who inhabited the spacious strath spread out beneath his feet. The burdensome pomp of royalty was gladly thrown aside, and, disguised as "The Gudeman o' Ballengeich," he enjoyed for a time the rude society of the humblest of his subjects. The beautiful prospect of mountains and vales brought tears to Queen Mary's eyes. When at the time of the Prince's baptism she stole away with an aching heart from the presence of unsympathetic guests and gazed in the direction of the Lake of Menteith, she doubtless recalled how as a little child she had been carried from Stirling to Inchmahome, and she must have felt a passionate longing to recover the golden girlhood days that she might live again through the happy years in France, and make a new beginning to her reign as Scottish Queen. James VI., on the whole, preferred the view towards the east and south to that in the direction of the Highlands. The peace-loving monarch realised that disturbed as was often the state of Lowland Scotland, it was a tranquil part of his realm compared with the region of mountains and glens. A sight of the purple peaks sometimes made him shake his head as he thought of the wild Macgregors and other kilted warriors, and felt that the day was not near at hand for their swords to be turned into ploughshares.

So striking is the beauty and range of the scenery which is displayed before the observer, that even a practical man of affairs of the sixteenth century could not refrain in a business document from expressing his admiration of the view. This was Sir Robert Drummond of Carnock, who, as Master of Works under James VI., drew up a report in 1583 on the condition of the buildings of the castle. His *Inventory*, which is preserved in the Register House at Edinburgh, recommends that the west-quarter of the Palace be pulled down and rebuilt to a height sufficient to make it command the four cardinal points, "by reason it will have the most pleasant sight of all the four airts: in special Park and Garden (deer therein), up the rivers of Forth, Teith, Allan and Goodie to Loch Lomond, a sight round about in all parts, and down the river of Forth where there stands many great stone houses." This project of Drummond's was not carried out, probably because of the greatness of the expense. The buildings were doubtless put in repair, but the west side of the Palace remains in the unfinished state in which it was left by the workmen of James V.

The visitor who has knowledge and appreciation of Stirling's majestic past will leave the castle with a sense that he has existed long before his present life, or with a feeling that the hands of the Clock of Time have gone back and have counted the years again. The early kings, such as William the Lion, Alexander III. and Robert the Bruce, will seem to have passed like ghosts before him, but he will almost persuade himself that he has seen the Regent Morton in the flesh, crossing from the Palace to the Parliament Hall, and George Buchanan, old and infirm, ascending the stair to the schoolroom in the Keep. It may be that he will fancy he has seen some other outstanding figures belonging to the past, for Stirling Castle is not given over to the shades of one or two personalities. A building may be visited by pilgrims on account of its memories of one great individual. It is Queen Mary's presence that dominates still the deserted chambers at Holyrood and Craigmillar, and that gives Loch Leven Castle the glamour which its other associations have failed to impart; but although the famous Queen of Scots spent many days at Stirling, the castle is so wealthy in romantic history that the elsewhere preeminent personality here takes its place side by side with other figures and does not occupy the forefront of the pageant of the shades.

Chapter Nine - Stirling's Position with Regard to Other Castles

Scotland, never having been conquered since the Scots themselves overcame the Picts, does not possess that type of castle that victorious invaders have been obliged to erect throughout their newly-won regions in order to keep the native races in subjection. Soon after the Norman Conquest, massive, square-built strongholds were raised in different parts of England for use as houses for feudal barons and as bulwarks against Anglo-Saxon insurrections. Rochester, Richmond and other well-known castles date from the period of the Norman kings. Scotland, again, has not many strongholds of the great Edwardian style, like those which make such conspicuous landmarks in Wales and the neighbouring English counties. Edward I. had never a firm enough hold upon the northern land to enable him to do more than strengthen some of the existing fortresses. Bothwell, Kildrummy and Lochindorb bear witness to the English monarch's influence, but they cannot rightly be classed as real Edwardian castles.

Although the strongholds of Scotland are, on the whole, of smaller dimensions than the castles of the adjoining kingdom, yet in her bestowal of sites suitable for fortresses, Nature has dealt more generously with the former than with the latter country. Each of the Castles of Edinburgh, Stirling and Dumbarton holds a commanding position upon a precipitous rock. The main incidents in Stirling's history, as compared and contrasted with those of the two sister strongholds, form the subject matter of this chapter.

Dumbarton differs from Stirling and Edinburgh in that it was prominent as a dwelling-place of princes before the other castles emerged from the haze of tradition. From the time of the departure of the Romans until the middle of the ninth century, Alclyde or Dumbarton was the capital of the independent British Kingdom of Strathclyde; but the union of the Scottish and Pictish nations in 844 proved too strong a coalition for the more southerly race to withstand. Stirling and Edinburgh cannot lay claim to any certain history during this early period. Yet the fairly-well-authenticated tradition of St. Monenna having founded chapels on the three great rocks in question links the castles together near the time of Strathclyde's loss of freedom.

The hard days of the War of Independence brought the strongholds roughly into line. Stirling, of course, on account of its pre-eminently favourable position for military strategy, received more attention from both English and Scots than either of the other castles. All three garrisons were forced to surrender to Edward I. in 1296, but while Edinburgh and Dumbarton remained in English keeping for many years subsequent to the Battle of Dunbar, Stirling changed hands again and again before its memorable surrender to Bruce after the Battle of Bannockburn. Yet, although defiant Snowdon bore the brunt of the struggle for national freedom, a more heroic feat of arms than any performed at Stirling took place in this war at the Castle of Edinburgh. Thomas Randolph with a few picked men, guided by a soldier who knew a dangerous track on the northern face of the rock, climbed the cliff on a dark night, while a feint attack was made at the principal gate, and won the stronghold for Scotland and the Bruce. In a later century, a somewhat similar deed of daring was successfully carried out at Dumbarton. In the early days of James VI., when the country was divided between the King's partisans and his mother's, Crawford of Jordanhill led a party up the rock at the place where it was highest, and took the slumbering garrison of the Queen completely by surprise. During the escalade, a member of the adventurous band was seized by an epileptic fit, but Crawford, undismayed by the untoward event, tied him to the scaling-steps upon which he happened to be standing, and by turning the ladder round made way for the others to ascend. Again, no tale of cunning strategy falls to be related of Stirling, such as that which describes the capture of Edinburgh in the second portion of the War of Independence. After the Battle of Halidon Hill, both castles passed into English keeping, but Sir William Douglas, the Knight of Liddesdale, recovered Dunedin by an artful ruse. Having sent to the gate a few of his warriors disguised as merchants with provisions, he lay with his main force concealed near the rock. The porter, glad to take in food for the garrison, admitted the crafty Scots, whereupon they threw down their bundles in the entrance to prevent the fall of the portcullis, and, having killed the porter, blew a horn to summon their companions. Douglas and his men rushed up the hill in time to support their countrymen against the on-coming garrison. A sharp conflict followed, in which the English, taken thus at a disadvantage, were defeated with heavy loss of life.

Yet although romantic exploits were of commoner occurrence at Edinburgh than at Stirling, at the latter fortress deeds of stout endurance and of daring brought renown to the warriors of Scotland. The famous siege of 1304, which resulted in the castle's being captured by Edward of England, reflected more credit on the defenders than on the attacking army. In spite of the King's largest and most modern military engines, supplied with all the ammunition which the Tower of London could provide, in spite of the advice and skill of his most experienced knights, in spite of the steady reduction in the food stores of the castle, the valiant Sir William Oliphant and his rapidly-diminishing garrison maintained a resistance for more than thirteen weeks. Some thirty years later, as an earlier chapter records, when the castle was again in English hands, the Scottish knight named Keith, in attempting to follow Randolph's great example, climbed up Stirling rock, but a missile from above caused him to lose his foothold and he met his death by falling on his spear; and as late as the siege of 1746, it will be remembered, some impatient Highlanders tried unsuccessfully to scale the dangerous cliff.

Stirling's proudest boast, however, is that the Battle of Bannockburn was fought for its possession. To save Scotland's most valuable fortress, Edward II. in the course of a year collected the largest English army that had ever taken the field. Bruce, in order to checkmate his opponent, faced the enormous invading host with the prize of the conflict at his back. No garrison at Edinburgh or Dumbarton had ever an opportunity of gazing from the ramparts on such a fight as that which took place outside the walls of Stirling. It is not given to many castles to be the object of a battle affecting the destinies of two nations, a battle that must be reckoned as one of the decisive engagements of the world.

Both Edinburgh and Stirling Castles stand out darkly in the annals of the princely House of Douglas. In one king's reign two chiefs of that great family were suddenly done to death when expecting courteous treatment in their sovereign's own halls. The Earl who perished at Edinburgh, although a youth of sixteen years, was regarded by William Crichton, who had made himself chief man of affairs during James II.'s minority, as a danger to the peace of the realm. Crichton invited him to come with his young brother to Edinburgh, to enjoy the companionship of the boy king and to assist in the government of the country. Deep treachery, however, lurked behind the festivities which were held to greet the Earl's arrival. At the close of a banquet given in honour of the Douglases, a bull's head was set upon the table—a proceeding which the Earl at once recognised as a sign of his approaching death. A hasty trial was held for form's sake, and thereafter the two youths were led to execution in spite of the earnest remonstrances of James. When at Stirling in later years this James of the Fiery Face drew his knife in his rage at another Earl of Douglas, he would have done well to have recalled, even in that moment of anger, the terrible scene of his boyhood at Edinburgh, and to have paused in horror at the thought of another royal castle's being stained with the Douglas blood.

Down to the time of the Union of the Crowns, and even later, Stirling Castle remained a royal residence, but the middle of the fifteenth century saw the beginning of a change in Edinburgh. Instead of taking up their abode in the fortress of Dunedin, the kings preferred to live in the valley with the canons of Holyrood Abbey. By the end of the century, the foundations of the palace had been laid, and thereafter the castle as a dwelling-place fell rapidly in the favour of the sovereigns of Scotland. A hundred years before the building of Holyrood Palace, however, a change of a different kind had taken place. Edinburgh having become by far the largest and most important town, English generals seldom penetrated into the heart of the country, deeming the sack of the capital the worst evil they could inflict. But for more than two centuries before the Union of the Crowns the only wars which troubled Stirling were those which Scots themselves stirred up when they found themselves at variance with their rulers. Dumbarton, again, lay open to invasion only from the sea, but this route was made use of by the traitor Earl of Lennox, when he sailed in the pay of Henry VIII., though he failed to induce the patriotic garrison to hand over to the English King the castle of which the Earl himself was governor and practical owner as well.

Henry VIII. was aware of the advantage of a western gate into Scotland. When Queen Mary was scarcely one year old, he audaciously proposed, in his scheme for uniting her with Edward, his heir, that she should be sent to England for her education, and that English garrisons should hold the castles of Edinburgh, Stirling and Dumbarton. The King therefore looked upon the fortress on the Clyde as one of Scotland's three most important strongholds, thus differing from an earlier Henry, who did not demand Dumbarton in the Treaty of Falaise, but stipulated for three Border castles along with Stirling and Edinburgh.

All three rocky strengths have been used as prisons for disobedient subjects of the Crown, but the stories of captives' romantic escapes almost all belong to Edinburgh. Although MacDonald of Gigha, in the reign of James VI., burst out of the castle on the Clyde, Dumbarton's as well as Stirling's walls seem to have been more formidable obstacles than the barriers of the capital fortress; or else it is a coincidence that Edinburgh's prisoners have been gifted with more guile than the others. Certainly the Duke of Albany and the ninth Earl of Argyll escaped by relying upon cunning. Albany, brother of James III., was ordered into ward by his sovereign on a charge of plotting against the Throne. He was able, however, to make good use of the help which his friends afforded. Wine was sent to him, along with which a rope was secretly conveyed. Albany invited the captain of the castle and one or two men to supper. The royal prisoner and his attendant refrained from drinking, while the guests consumed the liquor. At length the Duke and his varlet overpowered their helpless guardians, and having slain them, threw their bodies on the fire. Without delay the master and servant made their way to the edge of the rock. The wall was apparently easily climbed, and the rope was securely fastened. It was found, however, to be too short until Albany had added the sheets from his bed. Next morning this dangling line amazed both garrison and townsfolk, while the Duke was enjoying the fresh air of the Firth as he sailed for safety to France.

Two centuries later the Earl of Argyll, who suffered imprisonment for his Protestant principles, made good his escape by walking through the gateway disguised as a lady's page. Mackenzie of Kintail, Lord Maxwell and others found opportunity at different times to break from Edinburgh Castle and gain their liberty by scrambling down the rock.

Stirling more often than the other two castles has been sought by kings as a tower of refuge. When the party of the Comyns, in Alexander III.'s minority, stealthily carried the King from Kinross, it was to the fortress above the Links of Forth that they bore their rescued charge. The faction favouring England, from whose power the sovereign was snatched, did not attempt a counter-surprise; but although the walls of the castle secured Alexander's person, for a number of nights he must have quivered in his bed lest his former guardians should attempt to storm the fort. It was to Stirling in a later century that James V. took headlong flight when bolting from the exasperating tutelage of the Douglases. Like his early predecessor, James for many nights lay trembling on his couch. The Douglases, he knew, could command a large following. They were bold enough and disloyal enough to attack their King in his castle. When the wind groaned round the turrets and the gables he must have started from his restless sleep, thinking that his enemies were thundering at the gate. Still, he was now a free King, and he soon felt secure in the homely castle that had sheltered him from kidnapping nobles in the early years of his life.

Stirling was held to be the safest place of residence for James V.'s daughter, the child Queen Mary. In this case grasping nobles were not so much to be feared as King Henry VIII. of Eng-

OLD BUILDINGS IN UPPER SQUARE.

land. Edinburgh lay too near the Border, and was subject to devastation at the hands of the English soldiers, while the ruthless Tudor's agent, the Earl of

Lennox, was ever seeking to capture Dumbarton. The death of the dreaded Henry did not put an end to Scotland's fears. The "Black Saturday" of Pinkie soon followed, and although the child Queen remained in innocent happiness, not realising that for her sake hundreds of her subjects had given up their lives, her mother and the Earl of Arran were filled with the greatest fear lest the victorious English soldiers should seek out the young sovereign of Scotland. At the height of their alarm the anxious guardians sent the little Queen to the borders of the Highlands; but Stirling, as it turned out, was a safe enough abode, and soon she was brought again within its friendly protection. Twenty years later, however, when Mary escaped from Loch Leven, Dumbarton and not Stirling was the goal towards which she pressed; but the Earl of Moray came up with her near Glasgow, and having defeated her troops at Langside, turned her course southwards to England. In the wars that

A CHIMNEY OF THE PALACE.

followed Queen Mary's flight Stirling became the centre of the young King's party, while Edinburgh and Dumbarton Castles were held for his captive mother. Dumbarton, as has been observed, was afterwards forced to capitulate, and later Edinburgh underwent a siege, which ended in its also falling to the winning side and in Queen Mary's ill-fated cause being irretrievably lost.

In the troubles of after days all three castles submitted to the Protectorate, but in the following century none of them changed hands when the Jacobite risings disturbed the peace of Scotland. Dumbarton lay out of the routes of the insurgents both in the Fifteen and in the Forty-five, though the Earl of Mar's chiefs at one time had made up their minds to seize it; but Stirling and Edinburgh could not be neglected in either of those campaigns. In the earlier rebellion the attempt to storm the latter fortress failed because the well-laid plans were badly carried out; and the former castle was saved from attack by Argyll's success in preventing Mar from crossing the River Forth. In the Forty-five both strongholds held out stoutly for King George, although the towns outside their gates made little or no resistance to the dreaded Highland clans.

As a fortress Stirling possesses a history which places it first among the castles of Scotland; as a palace its record entitles it to rank above Dumbarton and Edinburgh. Its double use as stronghold and as dwelling-place of kings gives it a unique position among the royal houses, for Falkland and Linlithgow were pleasure palaces erected upon the sites of ancient castles, and Holyrood was built as a kind of extension to a defenceless, low-lying abbey. Edinburgh Castle, it is true, was for centuries a seat of kings as well as a famous fortress, but long before the Stewarts took up residence in England the abbey-palace as a home had superseded the stronghold. In the sixteenth century Edinburgh Castle was preferred by royalty to Holyrood only in times of peril. Queen Mary moved up from the valley to the rock before giving birth to James VI., the Riccio murder having made her realise the danger of living at the palace.

There was never a Holyrood Palace at Stirling to rob the castle of any of its glory. Kings might have lived in Cambuskenneth Abbey instead of on the summit of the windy rock; but it did not seem good to James IV. or any other monarch to erect a royal house beside the convent near the river. At Stirling the much-beloved old castle underwent various changes as the centuries rolled on; and when, with the advance of time, the taste for luxury developed and the Renaissance style of architecture was introduced from France, the fortress, instead of ceasing to be occupied by royalty, was crowned with a richly-carved palace. Until Scotland was forsaken by her ancient line of monarchs Stirling remained as much in favour with the kings and queens as the palaces of Falkland and Linlithgow, which were almost unencumbered with a castle's fortifications.

Stirling Castle thus retained its hold on the affections of the Scottish sovereigns. It therefore stands out from its sister castles in that it kept its place as a royal residence beside the palaces of Falkland and Linlithgow, while Dumbarton became more of a noble's stronghold than a prince's seat, and while Edinburgh sank from its position as a monarchs' home to that of a mere garrison fortress. Stirling, to be sure, also fell from its high estate, but its humiliation was long delayed, and did not come until after the Royal Family had ceased to be domiciled in Scotland.

All down the centuries Stirling Castle has been a place of arms, but since royalty ceased to dwell under its roof soldiers have become its most important, and almost its only, occupants. After the Union of 1707 the British Parliament followed the Scottish Estates in maintaining a garrison in the fortress, as well as in Edinburgh and Dumbarton, but the statement often made that the Treaty of Union requires this arrangement to be kept up has no foundation in fact. The error possibly arose from the confusion of the Union Treaty with an agreement made by Scottish and English commissioners in 1641. This earlier set of articles contains a clause providing for the furnishing for military purposes of the Castle of Edinburgh and other strengths of the kingdom. Long before the Union was carried out this Treaty became null and void, for the Scottish Parliament in 1661 rescinded all statutes that had been passed since 1640. Stirling Castle is used to-day as barracks, but the Government is not bound by any treaty to maintain a garrison in the fortress.

Chapter Ten - Stirling Castle in Poetry

It was Nathaniel Hawthorne who said that it takes a great deal of history to make a little poetry. The record of Stirling Castle bears out this remark, although it might be maintained also that in the case of the grey bulwark overlooking the River Forth a great deal of history has oppressed and has tended to silence the sensitive Muse of Poesy. The ancient fortress has been mentioned in verses composed in different ages, but the romance and magic of the storied spot remained unrevealed by rhyming chronicler or bard until Scott wrote *The Lady of the Lake*.

Scotland is a country rich in ballad literature, and although nearly every part of the kingdom has produced folk-poems of merit, the Borders and Aberdeenshire have been the most prolific districts. The Forth, that "bridles the wild Highlandman" and that has upon its bank a famous castle-palace, cannot vie in minstrelsy with less important streams, such as the Yarrow and the Don.

The well-known ballad of "Young Waters," however, takes for its theme a Stirling episode. It seems to commemorate the death of Murdoch Duke of Albany's eldest son, Walter, who was executed on the Heading Hill in 1425 by order of James I. Ballads cannot be relied upon to adhere to the facts of a case. In course of transmission from mouth to mouth they acquire a more and more romantic cast, and romance does not always agree with sober history. The Walter Stewart known to historians was condemned to death by a jury of barons for the crime of robbery or brigandage; but the ballad of "Young Waters" assigns the jealousy of the King as the cause of its hero's execution.

YOUNG WATERS.

About Yule when the wind blew cool,
   And the round tables began,
O, there is come to our king's court
   Mony a well-favoured man.

The queen looked o'er the castle wa',
   Beheld baith dale and down,
And there she saw young Waters
   Come riding to the town.

* * * * *

Out then spake a wily lord,
    And to the queen said he:
"O, tell me, wha's the fairest face
    Rides in the company?"

"I've seen lord, and I've seen laird,
    And knights of high degree;
But a fairer face than young Waters'
    Mine een did never see."

Out then spake the jealous king,
    And an angry man was he:
"O, if he had been twice as fair,
    You might have excepted me."

"You're neither laird nor lord," she says,
    "But the king that wears the crown;
There is no knight in fair Scotland,
    But to thee maun bow down."

For a' that she could do or say,
    Appeased he wouldna be:
And for the words which she had said,
    Young Waters he maun die.

They ha'e ta'en young Waters,
    Put fetters to his feet;
They ha'e ta'en young Waters,
    And thrown him in dungeon deep.

"Aft ha'e I ridden through Stirling town
    In the wind baith and the weet;
But I ne'er rade through Stirling town
    Wi' fetters at my feet.

"Aft ha'e I ridden through Stirling town
    In the wind baith and the rain;
But I ne'er rade through Stirling town
    Ne'er to return again."

They ha'e ta'en to the Heading Hill
    His young son in his cradle;
And they ha'e ta'en to the Heading Hill
    His horse baith and his saddle.

They ha'e ta'en to the Heading Hill
　　His lady fair to see;
And for the words the queen had spoke
　　Young Waters he did die.

The slaughter of the Earl of Douglas by his sovereign has not been commemorated in any ballad, although the Douglas execution at Edinburgh formed the subject of some verses, of which only one has survived:

"Edinburgh Castle town and toure
　　God grant thou sink for sin,
And that even for the black dinnour
　　Erl Douglas gat therein."

The Stirling victim, however, was not an innocent sufferer, as were the youths who perished in Dunedin. In a sense he deserved his fate, for his plans of treachery to the Crown were deeply laid. His well-known guilt no doubt silenced the bards, even those of his own house; for while they could wax indignant and eloquent at the cruel treatment meted out to harmless boys, they could not sound the praises of one who, though wronged, was himself an evil-doer.

The rhyming chronicles dealing with Stirling Castle, although less worthy of being classed as poetry than "Young Waters," keep truer to history than that ballad. The plain style of Langtoft, an English writer who lived at the time of the War of Independence, may be seen from two of his lines referring to the siege of 1304:

"Thrittene grete engynes, of alle the reame the best,
　　Brouht thei to Striuelyne, the castelle doun to kest."

Wyntoun, the Scottish chronicler, who wrote in the early fourteenth century, tells his tale in an equally straightforward manner. Stirling comes under his notice many times, and in speaking of Robert the Steward's siege he says:

"The Wardane than fra Perth is gane
To Stryvelyne wyth off his ost ilkane,
That castelle till assege stowtly....
　　　　　　　　* * * * *
The Wardane has this castelle tane,
A wycht hows made off lyme and stane,
And set in till sa stythe a place
That rycht wycht off it-selff it was."

John Barbour, Archdeacon of Aberdeen, comes, as regards time, between Langtoft and Wyntoun; but he was no mere chronicler, he was a great epic poet. In his day there were men still alive who had fought under Robert I., and from the lips of some of those warriors he learnt the particulars of many of the incidents presented in his poem, *The Brus*. Barbour is at his best in battle scenes, which he describes with clearness and power, and in those deft touches by which he reveals the characteristics of the hero and his companions. As the Battle of Bannockburn was the greatest event in Bruce's life, and as the determination of two peoples to possess the Castle of Stirling was the cause of the mighty conflict, it cannot be said that the poem does not deal with Scotland's principal fortress. Yet the references to the coveted stronghold do no more than explain the story; they are neither descriptions of the place nor accounts of its previous history. Edward Bruce's siege, which brought about the battle, is of course mentioned in the poem:

> "Till Strevilling syne the vay he tais,
> Quhar gud schir Philip the Mowbra,
> That wes full douchty at assay,
> Wes vardane, and had in keeping
> That castell of the Yngliss kyng."

When the day is lost to England, Edward II. flees to the castle:

> "Bot Philip the Mowbra said him till
> 'The castell, schir, is at your will;
> Bot, cum ye in it, ye sall see
> That ye sall soyne assegit be.'"

To be judged fairly, Barbour must be read at great length, but a few lines from his account of Bruce's duel with De Bohun may serve as an example of his spirited style:

> "Schir Henry myssit the nobill Kyng;
> And he, that in his sterapis stude,
> With an ax bath hard and gude
> With sa gret mayn roucht hym ane dynt,
> That nouthir hat no helme mycht stint
> The hevy dusche that he him gaf,
> That he the head till harnyss claf."

Blind Harry, who collected traditions about Wallace and wove them into a poem in the days of James III., could not help referring to Stirling Castle; but his lines on the subject are not more interesting than Barbour's, and his work as a whole is inferior to that of his predecessor in the field of patriotic poetry.

It is difficult to believe that a Scottish poet could use hard words when writing of Stirling; yet when it suited him, William Dunbar could pen vindictive lines on the place. It was indeed the town more than the castle that roused the "makar's" displeasure, but the royal dwelling cannot be held to be exempt from the general condemnation. It must, however, be remembered that this dirge which Dunbar addressed to James IV. was composed for a special purpose; the poet's real opinion of Stirling was probably on the whole a favourable one, just as his love for Edinburgh, expressed in this same work, seemed to turn to hatred when he wrote his satire on the capital. James, in one of his penitential moods, had gone to pray with the Observantine Friars at Stirling; consequently the Court at Holyrood grew dull, and Dunbar felt the dreariness as much as the nobles and ladies. As time went on, and the King continued to remain in seclusion, the court-poet, to relieve his feelings, wrote his "Dregy" or dirge, of which some of the lines are as follows:

"We that ar heir in hevins glory,
  To you that ar in purgatory,
  Commendis ws on our hairtly wyiss;
  I mene we folk in parradyis,
  In Edinburcht with all mirriness,
  To yow of Striuilling in distress,
  Quhair nowdir plesance nor delyt is
  For pety thus are Apostill wrytis.
                   * * * * *

"And all the hevinly court devyne,
  Sone bring yow fra the pyne and wo
  Of Striuilling, every court-manis fo,
  Againe to Edinburghis ioy and bliss,
  Quhair wirschep, welth and weilfar is,
  Pley, plesance and eik honesty;
  Say ye amen, for cheritie."

Dunbar has another poem dealing with Stirling called "Ane Ballat of the Fenzeit Freir of Tungland." The subject of this set of verses is the foreigner John Damian, who imposed in many ways on the credulity of James IV. The experiment in flying, spoken of in an earlier chapter, is made fun of by the poet, and although he does not mention Stirling in his account of the impostor's attempted flight, it is known that the castle was the scene of the exploit. By stating that the poem records the happenings of a dream, Dunbar leaves himself free to indulge his taste for exaggeration. The following are the last three verses of the ballad:

"He tore his feedreme [100] that was schene,
  And slippit owt of it full clene,
  And in a myre, up to the ene,
    Amang the glar did glyd.
  The fowlis at all the feathers dang,
  As at a monster thame amang,
  Quhill all the pennis of it owsprang
    In till the air full wyde.

"And he lay at the plunge evirmair,
  Sa lang as any ravin did rair;
  The crawis him socht with cryis of cair
      In every schaw besyde.
  Had he reveild bene to the rukis,
  They had him revin all with thair clukis:
  Thre dayis in dub amang the dukis
      He did with dirt him hyde.

"The air was dirkit with the fowlis,
  That come with yawmeris and with yowlis,
  With skryking, skrymming and with scowlis,
      To tak him in the tyde.
  I walknit with the noyis and schowte,
  So hiddowis beir was me abowte;
  Sensyne I curss that cankerit rowte
      Quhairevir I go or ryde."

To Dunbar's younger contemporary, Sir David Lyndsay, Stirling was not "every court-manis fo," but was the ideal place of residence in which to spend the summer months. The words which he put into the mouth of James V.'s "papyngo" or parrot were doubtless in agreement with the poet's own views:

"Adew, fair Snawdoun! with thy touris hie,
    Thy Chapell Royall, park and tabyll rounde!
  May, June and July walde I dwell in thee,
    War I ane man, to heir the birdis sounde,
    Quhilk doith agane thy royall roche resounde."

Lyndsay knew Stirling well, for he was principal attendant upon young James V.:

"Thy purs master and secreit Thesaurare,
    Thy Yschare, aye sen thy natyvitie,
  And of thy chalmer cheiffe Cubiculare."

And as Stirling was the home of the King's boyhood, it was in the castle that the usher romped with his royal charge and for his amusement played upon the lute:

"Quhow, as ane chapman beris his pak,
  I bure thy Grace upon my back,
  And sumtymes, stridlingis on my nek,
  Dansand with mony bend and bek,
  The first sillabis that thow did mute
  Was PA, DA LYN, upon the lute."

Pleasing pictures Lyndsay gives in "The Dreme" and in "The Complaynt to the King" of this happy comradeship with the boy sovereign. In after years, when he was free from the Douglas tutelage, James rewarded his old companion by bestowing upon him the honour of knighthood and making him Chief Herald, or Lord Lyon King of Arms.

Stirling Castle, when Sir David Lyndsay knew it, was a pile of stately buildings and the home of a gay Court. Two-and-a-half centuries later, when Robert Burns visited Stirling, the ancient seat of kings, long deserted by its royal owners, was tumbling fast into ruins. Carried away by anger at the neglected state of the castle, the poet broke out into these lines, which he scratched on the window-pane of an inn at Stirling:

"Here Stuarts once in glory reigned,
    And laws for Scotland's weal ordained;
    But now unroofed their palace stands,
    Their sceptre's sway'd by other hands.
    The injured Stuart line is gone,
    A race outlandish fills their throne—An idiot race to honour lost:
    Who know them best despise them most."

Burns afterwards felt that his words were too severe, and so, when he returned to Stirling, he broke the inscribed pane of glass. He was too late, however, to prevent the lines from being circulated far and wide.

Burns's junior contemporary, James Hogg, the Ettrick Shepherd, could not refrain from breaking out into verse in praise of Stirling Castle:

"Old Strevline....
                    ... I love thee more
    For the grey relics of thy martial towers,
    Thy mouldering palaces and ramparts hoar,
    Throned on the granite pile that grimly towers
    Memorial of the times, when hostile powers
    So often proved thy steadfast patriot worth;
    May every honour wait thy future hours,
    And glad the children of thy kindred Forth,
    I love thy very name, old bulwark of the North."

After Burns's visit the buildings did not long remain in the roofless condition which had called forth his bitter ejaculation, for when Dorothy Wordsworth saw the castle sixteen years later—in 1803—the place had been put in order, although it had suffered much disfigurement, and she remarked that the whole building was in good repair. William Wordsworth accompanied his sister to Stirling, and it might have been expected that such a striking object as the castle would have been made the subject of one of the poems which he wrote as memorials of this tour in Scotland. But Wordsworth never could feel the romance of a medieval fortress. Towers and battlements, studded doors and grated windows, spoke to him of only cruelty and oppression. The actions of peasants excited his sympathy, but not the deeds of feudal kings and warriors. He closed his eyes and ears to Stirling's past, and regarded the rock merely as a favourable view-point. He mentions the castle in "Yarrow Unvisited," but only as the place whence he had surveyed the windings of the River Forth:

> "From Stirling Castle we had seen
>> The mazy Forth unravelled;
> Had trod the banks of Clyde, and Tay,
>> And with the Tweed had travelled;
> And when he came to Clovenford,
>> Then said my *winsome Marrow*,
> 'Whate'er betide, we'll turn aside,
>> And see the Braes of Yarrow.'"

A different type of man from Wordsworth was his friend, Sir Walter Scott. Wordsworth enjoyed tranquillity and contemplation, Scott rejoiced in activity, and would have liked to be a soldier. The feudalism that repelled the Lake Poet attracted the Wizard of the North. An ancient castle reminded Sir Walter of deeds of self-sacrifice and of the joyous days of chivalry, and even in the stories of bloodshed and crime, from which Wordsworth turned in horror, Scott was able to find a strain of poetry and romance.

The plot of *The Lady of the Lake* is based on James V.'s well-known habit of wandering through his kingdom in disguise. In the poem the monarch calls himself not "The Gudeman o' Ballengeich," but "Fitz-James, the Knight of Snowdoun,"

> "'For Stirling's tower
> Of yore the name of Snowdoun claims,
> And Normans call me James Fitz-James.'"

The scene of the sixth canto is laid in Stirling Castle, while in the earlier parts of the poem the shadow of the fortress is made, as it were, to fall across the country of Clan Alpine. The Highlanders of the Lennox and Menteith could never quite forget the royal stronghold on the Forth. Its far-away outline was a warning and a check even to the restless Macgregors. Had the clans been able to join their forces they might have ventured to defy the castle; but feuds amongst themselves prevented combined action. A league such as Scott makes Roderick Dhu propose between his clan and the Douglases must sometimes have been thought of by actual Highland chiefs, and no doubt several kings half expected to be surrounded at times by Highlanders at Stirling:

"'To Douglas, leagued with Roderick Dhu,
Will friends and allies flock enow;
Like cause of doubt, distrust, and grief,
Will bind us to each Western Chief.
When the loud pipes my bridal tell,
The Links of Forth shall hear the knell,
The guards shall start in Stirling's porch;
And, when I light the nuptial torch,
A thousand villages in flames
Shall scare the slumbers of King James!'"

Any plans the Highlanders may have made for attacking the sovereign on his lofty rock were never carried out, but, on the other hand, chiefs such as Roderick Dhu were frequently warded in the castle. Scott was not drawing wholly upon his imagination when he imprisoned the head of a clan in the fortress, and when he made the outlawed Douglas appear before James V. in the Royal Park of Stirling. The pathetic story of Archibald of Kilspindie vainly endeavouring to catch a kindly look in the monarch's eye is elaborated in the poem, though Scott does not intend his Douglas to be identified with the historical character. The poet makes his outlawed hero exclaim as he glances up at the grim fortress "Where stout Earl William was of old"—the fortress that seemed likely to be the scene of his imprisonment and death:

"'Ye towers! within whose circuit dread
A Douglas by his sovereign bled.'"

But in order that the tale might be brought to a happy conclusion, a reconciliation is made to take place between the King and the man whom he had refused to own as a subject. Neither Scott nor Theodor Fontane, in his German ballad called "Archibald Douglas," could bear to leave the Kilspindie story as history records it.

Poets of the minor order, such as Hector Macneill, William Sinclair and John Finlay, have written lines on Stirling and the historical events connected with it, but they have not succeeded, as Scott has done, in bringing the castle's past back to life. Such a great past requires a great poem, and *The Lady of the Lake*, although dealing with only six days of James V.'s reign, makes clear Stirling's position as a palace, a fortress and a prison, and shows the significance of its geographical situation—in the Lowlands and yet near the verge of the Highlands. Walter Scott, both an antiquary and a poet, understood better than any other author the history as well as the romance of the "grey bulwark of the North."

Notes

[1] *Itinerary*, p. 311.
[2] Skene, *The four Ancient Books of Wales*, I. p. 85. O'Hanlon, *Lives of the Irish Saints*, VII. p. 60.
[3] Johnston, *Place-Names of Stirlingshire*, p. 60.
[4] *Poems of William Dunbar* (Scottish Text Society), II. p. 115.
[5] *Registrum de Dunfermelyn*, p. 8.
[6] Rymer, *Fœdera*, pp. 30, 31.
[7] *Registrum de Dunfermelyn*, pp. 38, 39.
[8] *Liber Pluscardensis*, VI. xliiii.
[9] Fordun, *Gesta Annalia*, LII.
[10] *Exchequer Rolls*, I. p. 24.
[11] *Exchequer Rolls*, I. p. 24.
[12] *Itinerary of King Edward I.* II. p. 280.
[13] Bain, *Calendar*, IV. p. 381.
[14] Bain, *Calendar of Documents relating to Scotland*, II. p. 518.
[15] Stevenson, *Documents Illustrative of the History of Scotland*, II. p. 481.
[16] Stevenson, II. p. 494.
[17] Rymer, *Fœdera* (London, 1816), I. p. 963.
[18] Rymer, I. p. 964.
[19] Bain, *The Edwards in Scotland*, p. 43.
[20] Mackenzie, *The Battle of Bannockburn*, pp. 67, 81.
[21] *Cal. of Docs. relating to Scotland*, III. p. 367.
[22] *Rotuli Scotiae*, I. *passim*.
[23] *Calendar of Documents relating to Scotland*, III. p. 252.
[24] *Registrum Magni Sigilli*, p. 125.
[25] *Exchequer Rolls*, IV. p. 591.
[26] *Treasurer's Accounts*, IV. p. 134.
[27] *Ibid.* p. 137.
[28] *Treasurer's Accounts*, I. *passim*.
[29] *Letters and Papers of Henry VIII.* 2, I. p. 209.
[30] *Historical MSS. Commission Report, Mar and Kellie Papers*, pp. 11, 12.
[31] Godscroft (Ed. 1743), II. pp. 107, 108. *Diurnal of Occurrents*, p. 19.
[32] Knox, *History of the Reformation*, Book I.
[33] *Calendar of Scottish Papers*, I. p. 555.
[34] *Calendar of State Papers (Foreign)*, 1561–2, p. 353, note.
[35] *Calendar of State Papers (Foreign)*, 1564–5, p. 328.
[36] *Diurnal of Occurrents*, p. 105.
[37] Keith's *History*, I. p. xcviii.
[38] Melville's *Memoirs*, pp. 167, 169 (Bannatyne Club).
[39] Melville's *Memoirs*, pp. 171, 172.
[40] Birrel's *Diary*, p. 6.
[41] *Diurnal of Occurrents*, p. 107.
[42] *Diurnal of Occurrents*, pp. 147–9.
[43] *Calendar of State Papers (Foreign)*, 1561–71, pp. 526, 527.
[44] Calderwood, III. pp. 139. 140. Spottiswoode, II. pp. 164, 165. *Historie of King James the Sext*,

pp. 90, 91. *Diurnal of Occurrents*, pp. 247, 248.

[45] *Diurnal of Occurrents*, p. 317.

[46] Tytler's *History*, VIII. p. 10.

[47] *Secret History of the Court of James I.*, II. p. 2.

[48] Melville's *Diary*, p. 48.

[49] Mackenzie, *Lives of Scots Writers*, III. p. 180.

[50] Irving's *Memoirs of Buchanan*, p. 166.

[51] *Ibid.*, p. 176.

[52] Bowes' *Correspondence*, pp. 6, 7. *Register of the Privy Council of Scotland*, III. p. 711.

[53] *Reg. of Privy Council*, III. p. 689.

[54] Calderwood, III. pp. 413, 414.

[55] Moysie's *Memoirs*, p. 22.

[56] Moysie's *Memoirs*, p. 25.

[57] Tytler, VIII. pp. 64, 65.

[58] Calderwood, IV. p. 25. Spottiswoode's *History*, II. p. 310.

[59] Birrel's *Diary*, p. 33. *Register of Privy Council of Scotland*, V. p. 165, *n.*

[60] Calderwood, V. pp. 343–5. Spottiswoode, II. pp. 455–6.

[61] Fraser, *The Chiefs of Colquhoun*, I. pp. 187–189.

[62] *Reg. Privy Council*, IX. p. 128.

[63] *Mar and Kellie Papers*, pp. 43–4

[64] *Ibid.*, p. 51.

[65] Birch, *Life of Henry, Prince of Wales*, pp. 66–7.

[66] *Ibid.*, p. 354.

[67] Birch, *Life of Henry, Prince of Wales*, pp. 75–6.

[68] *Privy Council Register*, VII. pp. 16, 580. 2nd Series, VIII. pp. 258–9.

[69] Calderwood, VI. *passim.*

[70] *Mar and Kellie Papers*, pp. 60–3.

[71] Balfour, *Historical Works*, II. p. 34.

[72] *Privy Council Register*, IX. p. 137.

[73] Calderwood, VII. p. 246.

[74] *Privy Council Register*, 2nd Series, IV. p. 380, V. pp. 17, 52–3.

[75] Balfour, II. p. 201.

[76] *Acts of Parliament*, V. p. 288.

[77] Balfour, III. p. 189.

[78] *Privy Council Register*, 2nd Series, VIII. p. 115.

[79] Balfour, IV. p. 250.

[80] Diary in *Scotland and the Commonwealth* (Scottish History Society), pp. 1–5.

[81] MS. in Bodleian Library.

[82] *Scotland and the Protectorate* (Scottish History Society), p. 368.

[83] *Acts of Parliament*, VII. p. 107.

[84] Nicoll's *Diary*, p. 300.

[85] Wodrow's *History*, II. p. 228.

[86] *Progress of James, Duke of Albany and York* (Edin. 1681).

[87] *Acts of Parliament*, IX. p. 82.

[88] Chevalier Johnstone's *Memoirs*, p. 87.

[89] Johnstone's *Memoirs*, pp. 90, 105.

[90] *Scots Magazine*, VIII. p. 42.

[91] *Exchequer Rolls*, VII. p. 452.

[92] *Exchequer Rolls, passim.*

[93] *Treasurer's Accounts*, IV. pp. 282, 526.

[94] *Treasurer's Accounts*, VII. p. 482.

[95] *Exchequer Rolls*, XIX. *passim.*

[96] *Stirling Archaeological Society's Transactions*, 1906–7, p. 123.

[97] *Register of Great Seal of Scotland*, II. p. 619.

[98] *Scotia Rediviva*, p. 476.

[99] Stevenson, *Documents*, II. p. 491.

[100] Coat of feathers.

www.ingramcontent.com/pod-product-compliance
Lightning Source LLC
Chambersburg PA
CBHW051848040426
42447CB00006B/748